If I Die Before
I Wake

A

Memoir

of

Drinking

and

Recovery

Barb Rogers

author of *twenty-five words*

Conari Press

First published in 2010 by
Red Wheel/Weiser, LLC
With offices at:
500 Third Street, Suite 230
San Francisco, CA 94107
www.redwheelweiser.com

Library of Congress Cataloging-in-Publication Data
Rogers, Barb, 1947–
  If I die before I wake : a memoir of drinking & recovery / Barb Rogers.
    p. cm.
  ISBN 978-1-57324-471-8 (alk. paper)
  1. Rogers, Barb, 1947– 2. Women alcoholics—United States—Biography.
  3. Women alcoholics—Rehabilitation—United States—Biography. I. Title.
  HV5293.R64A3 2010
  362.292092—dc22
  [B]
                    2009045111

Cover design by Maxine Ressler
Text design by Donna Linden
Typeset in Impressum, Neutra, and Perpetua
Cover photograph © Maxine Ressler

Printed in the United States of America
TS
10 9 8 7 6 5 4 3 2 1
The paper used in this publication meets the minimum requirements of the Ameri-
can National Standard for Information Sciences—Permanence of Paper for Printed
Library Materials Z39.48-1992 (R1997).

In memory of my friend, Cheryl Robinson

Contents

Acknowledgments

To all those friends of Bill who gave freely to me the messages that saved my life. To those who came after, to always remind me of where I've been. And to those who will continue to come, to pass the message of hope . . . I thank you, and will be forever grateful.

To Tom, my husband and friend. There are no words sufficient to express my love for you. You have truly been my greatest gift.

1

A Knock at the Door

A KNOCK AT THE DOOR, and the only constant in my life is gone. The one decent thing I ever did, my reason to go on, is no more. Music is playing on the radio, the cat is climbing the curtains, the dog is barking, the washing machine is humming and my son is dead. Everything is the same, and nothing is the same.

I wander through the shabby, rented house on the outskirts of Sullivan, Illinois, as if in a foreign land. In the kitchen, I fill a water glass half full of gin, drink it down in two gulps, and pour another. Glass in hand, I pace from one room to the next, touching the things he touched, looking at the things that belonged to him. Everything seems strange and out of place: the pool table and pinball machine my friend Tom gave him; the guitar propped up in the corner that he never learned to play well; his jacket hanging on its wooden peg. He will never touch those things again, and I will never touch him again.

The door to his bedroom is closed. Behind it, everything is as he left it, waiting for his return. I hesitate, drink the rest of my gin, and turn the knob. It appears so normal, like the typical room of a teenage boy. Hard rock posters are taped to the wall above the half-bed. On top of the chest of drawers are his plastic trophies; a troll doll with green hair standing on end, dressed in a tee shirt that says ROCK STAR in black letters; a wooden box for his treasures. A small, silver picture frame with no picture in it sits alone on the bedside table. He took his girlfriend's picture with him when he left. Everything is in its place—but Jon.

Angel, Jon's tiny black-and-white terrier, darts past me to leap on the bed she shared with him. I nearly lost her when Jon went away to the treatment center in Springfield—she stopped eating and moped around the house. Every day when the school bus pulled up, she'd run to the couch on the screened-in front porch, stand on her hind legs, and watch for him. It broke my heart because I knew just how she felt. I had always known loneliness, but nothing that compared to this.

Sitting on Jon's bed, I gather Angel into my arms, hold her close, and whisper into her ear, "He's not coming back." The flood of tears held closely in my broken heart lets loose.

Great sobs of sorrow erupt from the deepest part of me. I lie across his bed and push my face into his pillow, wishing I hadn't washed the bedclothes so I could smell him, hang on to a part of him. What will I do without him?

Hours later I open my eyes, hoping I have had one of my nightmares. I'm in Jon's bed, Angel curled up beside me, and it feels like someone beat me up. My eyes are red and swollen, my mouth and throat dry, and the truth sits on my chest like a stone. Angel jumps off the bed, ready to be let out and fed. Automatically I stumble from the bed, drag myself to the back door, and let her outside. I stand in the open doorway and watch the sun moving toward the horizon. I hear the birds chirping, a squirrel barking, cars whizzing by in the distance, and a siren. The world, and everything in it, is going on. My world has stopped.

Clamping my hands over my ears, I scream, "Stop!" Birds fly, the squirrel stops and stares, Angel runs past me into the house. But the sun continues to set, car engines still roar, and life goes on. Don't they get it—don't they understand that someone special is gone?

2

Alone

"IT ONLY TAKES ONCE," my mother often said. That seemed to be the extent of my sex education, and it normally took place after several beers and a few pills. She may have been drunk and hopped up on pills, but that didn't make her any less right.

Mom, my stepdad (who used to be my uncle), my brother, and I moved to Scottsdale, Arizona from Mattoon, Illinois the year I started junior high school. Mother's rare lung disease, fungal in nature, required a dry climate.

As with many new Westerners, we took up horseback riding. That's where I met "him"—at the riding stables. One might have thought the smell of crap in the air would have been a clue about the ill-fated liaison—but couple young, stupid, and desperate to get away from family with a tall, handsome, blue-eyed cowboy, and there was bound to be a spark. He smiled; I melted.

I had left a boyfriend in Illinois, but he was a child compared to the much older, rugged stranger I met in Arizona. Unsure at first about the horseback riding thing, I suddenly discovered a passion for it and spent as much time as possible at the stables. Jim was a pro baseball player from California, helping out at the stables for boarding fees. He paid attention to me. I felt like one of those heroines in a romance novel. We would fall in love. He would sweep me off my feet and away from the life I hated, and we would ride off into the sunset.

"Would you like to go on a night ride sometime?" Jim said one afternoon as I turned to leave. I wanted to throw myself into his big, strong arms, kiss him, and scream, "Yes, take me!" However, the heroines in my books wouldn't act that way. They would pick just the right moment for the first kiss. I gave him a coy smile and said, "I'd like that." Did I sound breathless? Could he see my heart beating through my thin, white cotton western shirt? It didn't matter. I had a date with the man of my dreams.

I begged, pleaded, and ultimately resorted to blackmailing my brother Bill with some unsavory information I had on him to lie to our mother and tell her we were going to a double feature at the drive-in. My brother, a year older than I with a driver's license, would be the key to my romantic evening beneath the stars and the beginning of a new life.

My dream date didn't go quite as expected. Jim got Bill—a nerd with thick glasses, a crew cut, and an extremely high IQ—drunk before the ride. He put him on an old nag and told him to follow us. Jim and I rode side by side toward the star-filled horizon. He took my hand in his. Then a strange sound caught our attention. I turned. My brother lay on the ground, floundering like a turtle on its back, his horse grazing nearby. Every time we put him back on the horse, he fell off again. We gave up. Jim threw a coarse saddle blanket on the ground. We sat close, his arm around my back, and shared our first kiss to the sound of Bill puking in the cactus.

In the months that followed, I slipped out of my window late at night, lied, skipped school, made up study dates, and used my brother whenever possible to get out of the house for stolen moments with Jim. One such afternoon, when things were getting pretty hot and heavy, he said, "I'm going back to California tomorrow." I burst into tears. He held me, professed his love, and said he would come back for me as soon as he got some things straightened out. I couldn't imagine life without him. He had my heart. He wanted my body. I gave him all that I had to give that day.

———

Hours turned into days, days into weeks, and weeks into months, but Jim didn't return. And neither did my period. I panicked—I had to get in touch with him. That's when I realized how little I actually knew about Jim. What baseball team did he play for? What city in California did he call home? Did he have any family there? When I'd asked for a phone number, he said it would be better if he got in touch with me. Looking back, I couldn't believe that in all the talks we'd had, he'd revealed nothing about himself.

The one thing I did know was that Jim's dad lived in one room of a broken down farmhouse on Baseline Road on the outskirts of Phoenix. We'd stopped there once, but just for a few minutes, and I had stayed in the car. I convinced myself that I had to find that house, Jim's dad, a way to tell him of his impending fatherhood. As soon as he knew, he would come back, and everything would be okay.

Still not old enough to attain a driver's license, I asked an older girlfriend, Linda, to drive me up and down Baseline in hopes that I would recognize the house. Mostly orange groves and flower farms, there weren't that many houses from which to choose. I found it on the third try. Jim's dad Mac was a weathered, aging cowboy with thick white hair that stuck out around a well-worn, stained, brown felt cowboy hat. He lived in a kitchen that smelled of saddle soap, cigarettes, and coffee. His whole life seemed to be contained in that one room. Rodeo posters adorned one wall, an unmade half-bed beneath, and several wooden pegs draped with assorted jeans, shirts, jackets, and hats. A metal kitchen table, several chairs with ripped Naugahyde seats, a floor lamp with no shade, and a potbelly stove with a tin coffeepot on top completed the look of the dwelling of a man who either chose to live a very basic life or had no money.

Mac motioned me to a chair at the table. He lit an unfiltered cigarette, sat across from me, and said, "What can I do for you?" I poured out my heart to this man, a total stranger who would someday be my child's grandfather. Wiping my tears, I begged for any information about Jim's whereabouts. He took a long draw on the cigarette, smashed it out in a jar lid, and said, "I don't know what to tell you. I don't know where he is or how to get in touch with him. He just shows up here sometimes."

The next "sometime" Mac spoke of occurred in February. For eight months I'd lived on hope, convincing myself that Jim had a good reason for not coming back. Some days were more difficult than others. I missed going to school, spending time with the few friends I'd made in Arizona, and acting like a kid. I passed my days as a babysitter, housekeeper, and laundress for Mrs. Scopaletti, who lived three blocks from our house with her husband and six children. The majority of my earnings went to Scottsdale Baptist Hospital to pay for the birth of my child. I was miserable. But when one day the phone rang and I heard Jim's deep, familiar voice, everything I'd gone through went right out of my mind. He had come. We would get married, have the baby, and be a family. The dream was alive.

———

I'd heard that what you don't know can't hurt you, but in my case that simply wasn't true. What I didn't know nearly killed me. I dressed in my best maternity outfit, stood next to Jim in front of a minister in my parent's living room, and exchanged vows with him. We ate cake. Jim took my hand, and we walked outside. I imagined he had a surprise for me. He did, but not what I thought. He said, "I'm not staying. I married you so the baby would have a name. I'll take care of you and the baby financially, but we can't be together. I'm too old for you. It would never work." He turned and walked away.

Stunned, I walked through the house to my bedroom, closed the door, and sat in the wooden rocker I would use for the baby. I couldn't cry. I couldn't think. I just sat there in numbed silence until my mother walked through the door. When I saw her, the tears came. "You're going to have to pull yourself together," she said. "Think of the baby."

My tears were replaced with anger. First, she and my stepdad tried to make me get rid of the baby. When I refused, my stepdad slapped me across the face. Later, after they threatened me with no help, financial or otherwise, they thought they could make me put the baby up for adoption. Determined, I went to work. Their last ploy was that they would take the baby. There was no way I would let them do to an innocent baby what they'd done to my brother and me.

"The baby?" I screamed. "You mean the baby you wanted me to kill? Or, the baby you wanted me to give away? No . . . no, the baby you think you're going to take from me? That baby?"

"You're hysterical. You need to calm down," my mother said.

I glared at her, hoping she could see the hate in my eyes. "He left. He married me, and then he left."

"Don't you get it, Barbara? Are you that stupid? He only married you to keep from going to jail for statutory rape."

Rape? "He didn't rape me!"

"For Christ's sake, he's twice your age. Do you really think he wants to spend his time with a teenager? He's a grown man. The law says when a man his age has sex with a child, it's rape."

"I'm not a child."

Mom hesitated with her hand on the doorknob, turned, and said, "No, you're going to be a mother. You better start thinking like one."

"Yeah, like you would know anything about that," I mumbled. She shot me a look. "What?"

"It doesn't matter," I said. No matter what I had to do, I wouldn't let my mother raise my baby.

———

Jon Luther Lewis, a miniature image of his father, made his entrance into the world on March 8. Overwhelmed with feelings I'd never experienced before, I cuddled the sweet-smelling, perfect, tiny bundle in my arms. "No one will ever take you away from me," I whispered into the small, shell-like ear. "I'll take you away from here. They'll never hurt you."

———

Fifteen years later and a week after the knock on the door, the harbinger of the news which is every mother's greatest fear, I stand at my son's grave. My dear son is in a box, under the ground. The choices I made killed him. I am alone.

3

The Letter

DAYS PASS BY AS IF IN SLOW MOTION. I'm not here. I'm somewhere on the outside of the world, watching through a haze. Is
that what it's like to be dead? If I kill myself, will I be reunited
with my son, or lie in the ground, forgotten? Who will be left
to remember my child or to mourn my passing? I pour a shot
of brandy into my coffee. How should I do it? It must be dramatic; something memorable. I could take poison, lie across
Jon's grave, leave a poignant note.

Angel is barking. It's the postman. If I don't get to the mail, she'll tear it up. I don't know why, but when the mail comes through the slot in the door, Angel just attacks. As a result, many of my bills are sent back shredded and taped together. It's a race to the door. The dog wins, grabs a flyer, and shakes it furiously while I gather the few envelopes. I thumb through the bills on the way back to the kitchen. If I don't kill myself, I'm going to have to go back to work soon. There's a letter from my brother at the bottom of the pile.

The irony of the situation doesn't escape me. My last link to my son is the brother I've been estranged from for many years. Mom may have been an alcoholic and a pill popper, but she held the family, dysfunctional as it was, together. When she died, the tentative hold we had on each other died with her. It's like a gunshot exploded and sent us all in different directions.

One more shot of brandy, and I'll read my brother's letter. I know I shouldn't be drinking this early in the day, especially after what happened to me before, but it's the only thing that keeps me from running screaming into the street. I pick up the letter, stare at it, and lay it down. I can't read it now. I need to get cleaned up, go to the restaurant, and find out if I still have a job. The bills aren't going to pay themselves.

In the shower, my tears mingle with the hot water stream-ing over my body. I wish the pure clean water could wash away my sins; that I could step from the shower with my insides as clean as my outsides. I've started my life over so many times— but never without Jon. Together, we'd overcome so much, and no matter what, we always had each other. Now I have no one. I turn the hot water off. Cold water hits me like a blast of icy air. I have to stop this. It's time to pull myself together.

Dry, dressed in jeans and a tee shirt, it's time for the dreaded daily ritual of hair and makeup. I hate the woman in the mirror, the one who works so hard at looking good on the outside, but who I know is ugly. Mom used to say I looked like something the cat dragged in. I fixed that by learning the skills of styling hair and applying creams and makeup, but no amount of makeup can conceal what lives within. Now, I truly feel like something the cat dragged in—a hopelessly struggling victim trapped in the jaws of a cruel world.

Ablutions completed quickly, I glance at the letter, gulp down another shot of brandy, pop a mint in my mouth, and I'm out the door. I pray to the car god that my old car starts. It's too hot to walk the two miles to the Red Fox Restaurant, although I've had to do it many times before. I don't have the energy today.

The big, gold-colored gas hog, which sits in my driveway more often than not—either because it won't run or I don't have gas money—starts on the third try. I let out a sigh. If I had a phone, life would be easier. But that's not going to happen. Jon ran up a huge phone bill before he left for treatment, and I still don't have it paid off. I yelled at him about it, said things I wish I could take back. I shift the car into reverse and quickly back out of the drive before my thoughts wander to that dark place.

I walk through the bar, waving at the bartender who is setting up for the day ahead, past the dining room, and into the kitchen where I spend my working hours as a cook. Wayne, the owner and my boss, is prepping for lunch along with the salad girl. They stop and stare at me, obviously uncomfortable. I've encountered that a lot lately. It only makes things worse. I force a smile. Wayne leads me to his office and says, "Do you need a couple more days?"

A couple more days isn't going to change anything. My son will still be dead. I will still be alone. "No, I need to get back to work." The mortuary gave me a thirty-day grace period. After that, I will be giving them a percentage of my check each week until my debt is paid. "I can come back tomorrow, if that's okay."

I start home, change my mind, pull into the liquor store drive-through, purchase a pint of gin, and head toward the country. I can't go home. The letter is there, waiting for me. Fear grips me when I think of opening it. What more can Bill tell me that I want to know? Jon is dead, hit by a truck and killed on Central Avenue in Phoenix. He'll never graduate from high school, go to college, get married, or have children. I will not have grandchildren . . . not ever. The tears come. I can't believe I have any left. I unscrew the lid of the pint bottle, take a healthy swig, and continue to drive over the hilly country roads until I find myself at the cemetery. It's the last thing I remember when I come to, face down, chilled from the damp grass, lying next to the mound of dirt under which my son's body lies.

I struggle to my feet, head throbbing, and brush the dirt and grass from my clothes. Picking up the empty bottle, I toss it into the trees surrounding the tiny cemetery and convince myself I must have been exhausted from not sleeping well—that I simply fell asleep. I won't accept any other explanation, least of all that I drunkenly passed out. I can't. However, doubts assail

me when I locate my car off the gravel drive, parked danger-
ously close to a headstone. What time is it? I have to get home
to let Angel out and feed her.

A darkness unique to the cloud-filled, summer storm sea-
son of Illinois descends as I approach the house. There are no
lights on. I hate the dark. It has never been my friend. Angel
rushes out the screen door as soon as I open it, barely making it
off the sidewalk to relieve herself. Poor little thing. How long
have I been gone? I flip light switches as I move through the
house to the kitchen, pour myself a big glass of cold water, and
drink it down. As I turn from the sink, I see the letter. My heart
sinks. I do not want to know the details!

Angel fed, I gather her into my arms, go to Jon's room,
lie down on his bed, and weep into Angel's soft fur until sleep
comes. The sound of sobbing wakes me. He's there. I can see
him. He's standing at the end of the bed. Blood is gushing from
his mouth. I scream. He disappears. I rush to the bathroom,
hang my head over the toilet, and everything in my stomach
erupts. It can't be happening. Not again! It's the same nightmare I started having after my tiny infant daughter, Nikki, died.
When it got so bad I was afraid to go to sleep, I sought help
from a doctor. He told me to drink a little brandy before I went
to sleep. It took more than a little, but it worked.

———

Maybe it's time to read the letter. At the kitchen table, I stare at
it for long moments. With shaking fingers, I rip it open. When I

realize I'm holding my breath in, I let the air out and watch the handwritten pages flutter as I unfold them. And then I read.

It's all there; all the details I don't want to know. Until I read that letter, I was able to remember Jon as he was when I left him at the treatment center. Now, the picture of his death is embedded in my mind. The memory of my prayer, that god-awful prayer I'd uttered when he ran away from the treatment facility, returns. I hadn't prayed since my babies were dying, since my mother shot herself. They had all died; the prayer hadn't worked. I should have known better. But, I did it. I said, "God, I can't take care of Jon anymore. Will you look after him?" A few days later, he was dead. I might as well have signed his death warrant.

Choking back the tears, I begin shredding the letter into strips and watching the pieces float to the floor. Everyone I ever cared for either hurt me, left me, or died, and this God that everyone was so sure was out there somewhere, helping people with their problems, didn't give a damn about me. My life had been shit from the beginning, and it always would be.

4

Memories

FLASHBACKS OR MEMORIES . . . I don't know anymore. What I do know is I can't walk back into that house again. I think of how mad I used to get when I came home from work to find Jon's dirty, stinky sweat socks in the living room floor. I'd scream at him. Now, I'd give anything to see them, smell that familiar odor, just to know he is there. I see him in every doorway, lying in the floor playing with Angel, on the couch picking at his guitar, shooting pool with his friends. But he's not there.

No matter how hard I try, my memories always end with him dead in the middle of the road, hit by a car, his neck broken.

Immediately, memories of holding my other dead children in my arms—and then having to let them go, that emptiness—flood my mind. Nikki, my tiny infant daughter, born when I was just seventeen, was a fighter. She amazed the doctors when she lasted as long as she did, considering all her physical problems: a hole in her heart and lungs not fully developed.

My second son, Ronny, came along nearly two years later. He looked just like Jon except he had dark hair and skin like mine. Bigger than Nikki, more developed, the doctors thought he would make it. I was sure of it. Each day I went to the pediatric floor to check on him where he'd spent his short life in a clear box, hooked up to monitors. Then one day he suddenly stopped breathing. Nurses fluttered around. They closed the curtain. A doctor rushed through the door. I couldn't catch my breath. I collapsed in a heap, and the next thing I knew, I came to in a hospital bed. The doctor told me that Ronny was dead.

The only time I ever got to touch my babies was after they were dead. They looked like they were just sleeping, their little bodies still warm. I flash back to the days my infant daughter and son died, holding their lifeless bodies in my arms, praying it wasn't true, that they would open their eyes and it would all be a big mistake. I wanted to pull them to my breast and run away, but I stood there in stone silence, my tears running over their tiny faces, and let them be taken away from me and put in the ground. A few years later, when I lost a child before he was born, I simply shut down, knowing that for some reason I wasn't fit to be a mother.

My husband blamed me. I blamed myself. If I'd taken better care of myself, it wouldn't have happened. He didn't need to keep telling me. I knew it.

I knew I was a bad mother then, and I know it now. If I hadn't dragged Jon around with me like we were a couple of gypsies, if I hadn't put him through all the drama that was my life, he wouldn't be in the ground like his brother and sister. I put him there as surely as if I'd snapped his neck myself, and I could no longer live in the house where we lived together, where my memories haunted every corner.

I have a place to go, a rented room in another woman's house. I like her. She owns a beauty shop where I worked as a nail girl, and we partied in the same crowd. The rent on my house is paid for a month, so I have time to see if this new living arrangement works out. Right now, I can't see past packing a few things, gathering up the dog, taking the cat to a friend's house, and getting the hell away from the constant reminders of my dead son.

Like Mary Jo, whose long blond hair is never out of place, who wears the appropriate clothes for every occasion, who looks good even when she's drunk, the house is perfect. Everything is like brand-new, everything matches, but it seems to lack any personal touches. My secondhand clothes and few personal items seem out of place, as do I. Maybe I'll get used to it. I have to try, because I have no place else to go. Except for Aunt Ruthie, who's married to Mom's brother and fighting the good fight against cancer, what family I have left has nothing to do with me.

The irony of the situation with my family hasn't escaped me. At age 26, after running off with another woman's husband and finding myself and Jon deserted in a hotel in another state with no money, no clothes, and no car, I did what I always did when I was in trouble. I ordered drinks up to the room and signed for them. The next thing I remember was waking up tied hand and foot to a bed in a mental hospital in Springfield, Illinois. Apparently, sometime during my drunken stupor, I had called my most recent ex-husband. He drove to Kentucky to get us, but unable to handle me any longer, turned me over to the medical community.

They'd locked me up with a bunch of crazy people! I wasn't nuts—I was just drunk. I decided not to cooperate, but was put through months of drug and shock therapy before they released me—with conditions. I had to agree to stay on my medications and go to therapy, for at least two years. With all the help the state of Illinois was willing to give me, I had an opportunity to turn my life around, a chance to be a better person and a better mother. Finally sober, which I hadn't been for any length of time since I turned 17, I threw myself into therapy with a local psychologist even as I flushed the medications that made me feel like a slobbering fool. My therapist suggested that I stay away from my family for the first year. When I told them that, they didn't take it well. One would think that when an out-of-control drunk gives up the booze and is trying to do better, her family might embrace her. Not mine. From that moment on, I had no family except for Aunt Ruthie, who'd never been a drinker.

It's Saturday morning. Mary Jo is at work. I have the house to myself. Still in my robe after a long soak in the tub, I dart to the window when I hear a car pull into the driveway and car doors slam. My heart stops for a moment. What the hell are they doing here? It's my mom's sister, Juanita, and her husband, an abusive beer-soaked truck driver who got me drunk when I was 19 and raped me . . . a secret shame that I will take to my grave. He'd convinced me that the rape was my fault, and if I ever told, it would destroy Juanita and their two boys. As I peek through the blinds, I see the back door of the car open. It's Aunt Ruthie. I consider hiding, not letting them in, but I can't do that to Aunt Ruthie. She is the one person throughout my childhood who treated me decently, who never called me names or hit me.

Pulling the lapels of the shabby robe close around my neck, I open the door. Uncle John swaggers past me, followed by Juanita. They reek of cigarettes and beer. Juanita pulls me to her. I stiffen. As soon as Ruthie steps through the door, I launch myself into her waiting arms. The little girl who so wanted to be loved, for someone to tell her everything would be okay, emerges from me, and the tears I normally swallow in front of others pour down my face. Suddenly, I realize the woman holding me is half the woman she used to be. I pull back, unable to reconcile Ruthie's weight loss and the thick salt-and-pepper hair reduced to thin straggling wisps of fine, nearly completely gray hair with the woman I had known. The chemotherapy has really taken a toll on her. She's dying, and she's consoling me. Making the excuse that I need to get dressed, I run to my bedroom.

Collapsed across the unmade bed, I push my face into the pillow. Strange sounds erupt from the deepest part of me. I can't do it. I can't lose another person I care about. I can't go out there and act like nothing is wrong. Why Aunt Ruthie? I don't know how she does it . . . smiles through her pain, all the while knowing she's dying. It's not like she's had a good life. Her husband, my mom's brother and a drunk who gambles and chases anything in a skirt, never treated her right. She raised their three kids in spite of him, working long hours at a shoe factory until she had a hump in her back from bending over a sewing machine. But still, she's loving, kind, and sober. I don't get it.

Ruthie steps through the door, perches on the side of the bed, and takes my hand in hers. I see tears glistening in her eyes. "Soon," she says, "I'll go and take care of your Jon, but you'll have to stay here and look after my kids. Can you do that?" Unable to speak, I nod, but in the deepest part of me, I know it's a lie. I'm the last person anyone would want looking after their kids. "You are more than you think," she continues. "God has a plan for you."

After some stilted conversation and a few snide remarks cloaked behind false concern for me from John and Juanita, the need for a drink drives them out the door. I'm sure they have a cooler of beer waiting for them in the car. I focus on Ruthie's face through the backseat window of the big Buick as they back out the drive. Will this be the last time I see her?

A plan for me? God? More than I think I am? What did she mean? Given her circumstances, how can she believe in a God, some imaginary plan? I puzzle over this. The shrill ring of the telephone brings me out of my reverie. It's the local sheriff. He's getting a group of people together to speak at schools and churches about drug and alcohol addiction. I owe him one because he identified Jon after I had his body flown home. I didn't think I could live through seeing another one of my children dead. He wants me to speak from a parent's point of view. I agree, but before I hang up the receiver I know it's a mistake.

———

"Another day in paradise," I say to the empty kitchen and pour myself a large glass of wine. It's going to be one hell of a day. I need to write a letter to the young man who killed my son with his truck. It wasn't his fault, and I want to tell him that there is no reason his life should be destroyed by what was clearly an accident. As I lay in bed awake last night, staring out the window at the stars and wondering where my son is, I considered what to say. I imagined how I would feel if I killed another person. I would wonder about him . . . who he was, what he was like . . . and then my answer came. Now, I pull pen and paper out of Mary Jo's desk.

When I'm dressed, the ready-to-mail envelope clutched in one hand, the phone rings again. I hesitate, then answer it. It's Tom, the last person in the world I want to talk to at this moment. I can't decide if he's a blessing or a curse in my life. I just know that since the age of 20 I haven't been able to get him out of my mind. Our on-and-off relationship for over ten years has been euphoric at some times and disastrous at others. Jon always adored him, and no man I was with since had measured up in Jon's eyes. But Tom had hurt me, and I can't take any more hurt right now.

"I have to go. I'm on my way out," I say, hang up, grab up Angel, and rush out the door. After a quick stop at the post office to mail the letter, I turn the old car onto the country road that leads to the cemetery.

I don't want to go home.
It's not my home.
I don't have a home.

I've never felt like I had a home. Ruthie's words play through my mind. Tom's face, with his pale blue eyes that seem to see into my very soul, flashes in front of me. I step hard on the accelerator. I can't make the turn. The car skids off the road. Angel is thrown to the floor. Stopped, stunned, I gather the little terrier into my arms and weep. She licks at my tears and wiggles out of my arms. The door open, she jumps from the car and darts through a stand of trees. I follow her into a wide, grassy clearing.

———

A fallen tree supports my back as I sit on the thick spongy grass, still damp from the early morning dew, and watch Angel explore, peeing here and there. Warm beams of sunlight combine with a cool breeze to relax me. Sliding down, my head resting on the log, I notice the leaves are beginning to change color. Normally, I love the fall in Illinois—the red, orange, and yellow painting the edges of the foliage. But today the fall leaves take me back to another day, another time many years before when I felt much like I do at this moment: like I wish I could simply close my eyes, drift away, and never return. I wonder why I didn't let go of that boat.

5

Holding On

IT WAS THE SUMMER OF 1955, the year I turned 8. It would be my last summer on the Kaskaskia River with Grampa Chaplin and his wife, Alma. And, as my mother had reminded me several times, I had no one to blame but myself. I was a stupid, ungrateful child. If I had a brain, I would take it out and play with it. A whipping at the end of a willow switch couldn't have hurt any more than knowing I'd messed up the one good thing left in my life.

To me, there was nothing better than life on the river. The old cabin sat on the banks of the Kaskaskia, next to the Thompson Mill covered bridge, with fields of corn behind it. Electricity was unnecessary; the cabin had oil lamps and a wood cookstove. A well with the coldest, best-tasting water I'd ever had, and a two-holer outhouse took the place of inside plumbing. There were no windows, only wooden flaps that could be pushed out and propped up with sticks. Daily life consisted of hunting, fishing, swimming (which passed for taking a bath), picking berries, drawing water, and gathering firewood for the stove where Alma prepared fabulous meals of fried catfish, potatoes, corn, and corn bread in heavy cast iron skillets. My mouth would water at the aroma of Alma's homemade bread and berry pies cooling near the window.

As each mile passed on the hilly, twisting dirt roads that led to the river, I felt all the worries of town leave me. There was no greater feeling than discarding the hated secondhand dresses that never seemed to fit quite right, not having to attend a school where I would never fit in, not listening to the drunken fighting between whoever happened to be at the house, and not dealing with parents who seemed to be angry at me most of the time. The river was where I wanted to be, and I imagined that someday, when I got older, I would go there and live out my life.

But all good things must come to an end, and for my brother and me, that end would happen the day my mother and her new husband, who used to be our uncle, came to fetch us at the river. The weather had turned cool after a hard rain a few days earlier. While Grampa and Bill went hunting squirrels, Alma heated a bucket of water on the stove, poured it into an old washtub set in front of the stove, and scrubbed me down good with lye soap and the wooden-handled scrub brush that when turned over could be used as a paddle. I'd tasted the hard side of it many times. Clean, dressed in bibbed overalls, a tee shirt, and the shoes I would be wearing for school that fall, Alma turned me loose with dire warnings about not getting dirty before Mom came to get us.

I walked along the riverbank, poking at things with a stick I'd found along the way, until I spotted the rowboat Grampa used to check the trout lines bobbing up and down in the swiftly running, swollen, muddy river. It called to me.

Cautiously, so as not to get dirty, I slipped down the bank, grabbed the rope attached to the boat that was tied to a tree, and pulled it in. I jumped on board. I loved to lie in the bottom of the boat, feel the rocking motion of the river, and daydream. However, daydreams didn't come that day. My mind drifted to what I'd be returning to in town. Mom had divorced my dad and married his brother, a mean man whom I couldn't please no matter how hard I tried, and Dad had remarried a large Jewish woman with a little girl who was everything I would never be. In her white, fluffy dresses with jet-black hair that was never out of place, she looked like one of those porcelain dolls I'd seen in catalogues. The first time I saw her sitting on my dad's lap, I wanted to hit her and rip off her pretty dress. *She* sure didn't look like something the cat dragged in.

Lying in the boat, my head propped up on one of Grampa's homemade life preservers, I stared at the tops of the trees swaying in the breeze. They were just starting to turn colors around the edges. One let loose and drifted on air currents until it landed on top of the water to drift away. I wanted to be that leaf, to drift away to another place, never to return to my life in town again. Would it drift all the way to the ocean? I'd never seen the ocean, but I had seen pictures of it at school.

Without a second thought, I slipped over the side of the rowboat. The water was cold, the current swift. One waterlogged shoe was dragged off, followed closely by the other. My wet bibbed overalls weighed me down, tugging me away from the boat. I could barely hang on to the side. I heard Alma calling my name. All I had to do was let go, but it felt as if my hands were frozen to the wood.

Alma grabbed the rope and pulled the boat into shore. Then she jumped in (which really surprised me because she couldn't swim), grabbed my arm, and in one swift motion, hauled me into the boat. I don't know if it was fear, cold, or the sight of Alma's bowed legs encased in rolled-down support hose and her long underdrawers showing as she fell backward—but I started to laugh, and I couldn't stop.

Back on solid ground, my laughter turned to tears as Alma shook me, hard, yelling that the devil was in me, that I was evil, and she'd see to it that I never came to the river again. I thought at that moment that I should have let go. I should have closed my eyes, let go of the boat, and drifted away.

———

Angel's barking brings me to the present. Rising to my feet, I realize I have to face one more day when I don't have the courage to let go, to give up my life, even if it's a life of misery. I've thought of so many ways to kill myself, but something has always held me back. While Jon was alive, I had a good reason. I didn't want to leave him feeling about me the way I felt about my mother. Now that Jon's gone, I don't know why I can't do it. It's certainly not because I think things will ever get any better.

It's a short drive to the cemetery. After brushing the leaves from Jon's grave and pulling a few weeds that have grown up around the stone, I settle on the ground and lay my hand on the cold marble. I miss him—his laugh, that crooked grin he got when he played a joke on me or said something witty. Most of all I miss his love. He's the one person in my life who loved me in spite of myself. Tom, the man I've been secretly in love with for over ten years, comes to mind. I thought he loved me—I don't know how many times he bailed me out of trouble, even paid for my divorces, paid to have Jon's body flown home from Arizona. But—and there's always a *but*—I can't be with Tom. Our relationship was always a disaster, and there is no reason to believe it wouldn't be again. I will not let him hurt me. I can't deal with any more pain.

Angel's on my lap, head hanging out the window, as I drive slowly back to town, to Mary Jo's house. There's an unfamiliar car in the driveway, so I park on the street. Inside, I notice her bedroom door is closed. It's confusing, but what she does, and with whom, is not my business. I start down the hallway toward my bedroom. Mary Jo calls my name. Outside her door, I acknowledge her. She tells me to come in. It must not be what I imagined it to be, I think. I open the door. There they are, Mary Jo and my lawyer, who's a married man, propped up on the bed, stark naked. They do nothing to hide their nudity.

I'm no prude, especially when I've had a few drinks, but it's like a train wreck—I don't want to look, but can't stop myself. Mary Jo pats the bed and invites me to join them. Stunned, I mumble a few words and back out the door, closing it behind me. I hear them laugh. In my bedroom, I lock the door, and with shaking hands, begin to stuff my belongings into the two bags I brought with me. It's time to go home.

6

Starting Over

IT'S A HOT SUNDAY IN JULY, nearly a year since life as I knew it changed. The house is closing in on me. I consider going up to the town square, to the air-conditioned shops, but I don't have money to spend and I can't stand being around other people. Another visit to the cemetery? No, I've got to stop going there. I don't want to stop remembering Jon, but knowing where he is, and the truth of what put him there, is too much. I might as well take a stick with me and beat myself up every time I stand over his grave.

I slip into a skimpy silver bikini I've had since we lived in Florida during one of my more disastrous escapades a few years earlier. Grabbing a towel, I pick up the folded lounge chair that hangs on a nail on the screened porch, set it up in the yard, spread the towel over it, and return to the house for supplies. I shuffle through the books on life after death stacked next to the couch, pick one, grab a pack of cigarettes and a spray bottle filled with water, and fix myself a Long Island iced tea over ice in a tall, frosted glass.

Stretched out beneath the large oak in my side yard, I pick up *Here and Hereafter* by Ruth Montgomery, but I can't focus on the words. I've read everything I can get my hands on about the spirit world, but I'm still not convinced that it exists. If I ever get any spare money, I'll invest in a television. I had a small, 19-inch one that I bought at a yard sale, but it broke. I miss the distraction. After lighting a Salem, drawing the hot smoke deep into my lungs, and finishing off half my drink, I begin to feel a bit better.

Eyes closed, a warm breeze blowing gently across my nearly naked body, my thoughts wander to what month it is. I can barely remember the past year. I know I went to work, cleaned the house, walked the dog, ate food, slept, but none of it seems real. Is this what my life will be like? The rest of my drink slides down smoothly. I gave up worrying about my drinking months ago. It's the only thing that gets me through the day, allows me to sleep through the night and face each new morning. And what does it matter now? A cold beer would taste good.

A long white tee shirt with Mickey Mouse dancing across the front of it covering my swimsuit, I jump in the car and head for the liquor store. At the drive-up window, I order a six-pack of Coors, my favorite beer, pay the man, and pull out. Is that black car following me? Who is it? The car doesn't look familiar. I'm being paranoid. I keep watching it in my rearview mirror. It's pulling into my driveway after me. I can't see the driver through the tinted windows. What the hell is going on?

The car door opens. A woman steps out. It takes me a few moments to realize I've seen her before. But where? She smiles, waves, and says, "Got a beer?" I'm standing there with a six-pack dangling from my hand. Of course, I've got beer. I nod. She approaches. A hand over my eyes to cut the glare of the sun, I finally recognize her. A long time ago, I don't recall when exactly, I went into a local bar just off the town square. It was packed, and the woman in my driveway was the only one working. I heard her say the help hadn't shown up, so I offered to help her. She refused curtly, and I left thinking she was a bitch. Why is she here now? She doesn't look mad, so I surely didn't do anything to offend her during one of my blackouts, like sleep with her husband or insult her.

"Do you remember me?" she says. "I'm Cheryl. We met—"

"I remember," I interrupt, remove my shirt, and take a seat on a lounge chair. When it comes to people, I don't like women as a rule. I had a couple of women friends—one cheated me out of money, and the other started rumors about me. I'm not looking for any new girlfriends.

Laughing, she says, "Sorry about that. It was a bad night. So, are you gonna offer me a beer or what?"

Curious, I pull two beers out of the plastic rings, hand her one, and pop the top on the other. As if she belongs here, she goes to the side of the house, picks up an old wicker chair, moves it next to my lounge, sits, and takes a sip of the cold beer. "I haven't seen you around for a while."

It's too expensive to drink in the bars. If I let men buy me drinks, they expect to be paid one way or another. Lately, I haven't been up to paying that price, except for a couple of times I went to town in a blackout and woke up in a strange bed, with some awful man I wouldn't give the time of day sober. "I don't get out much."

"You want to go out tonight?"

"With you?"

"Why not? There's a band at the Legion."

I consider my options. I can spend another night alone— just me and the dog, reading a book about what happens to people when they die, drinking as much as I can, and passing out. Or I can go dancing. I haven't been dancing in a long time. We don't have to become bosom buddies, but she would be another body to walk in with. If I meet someone interesting, I can dump her.

"Why not?" I concede.

"I'll pick you up at eight."

Second thoughts assail me as Cheryl's car pulls out of the drive. It's too late. I don't know her last name, have her phone number—or a phone, for that matter. I'll have to go.

The chair stowed on the porch, I go inside, put the rest of the beer in the refrigerator, telling myself I can't drink anymore because I need my senses about me tonight. Besides, I've already got a good buzz going. Cheryl'll be back in a few hours. I'll spend the time soaking in a bath, do something unique with my hair, and put together the best outfit I can find. If I'm going out, I'm going to look good. Cheryl is a striking woman, with her dark hair and green eyes, and I know she's a lot younger than I am . . . maybe in her twenties. I turned 31 in June. I won't allow her to show me up.

Standing on a chair, I review my image in the dresser mirror. In a pair of cutoff Levi shorts, a low-cut denim vest that emphasizes my cleavage and tanned skin, a pair of strappy sandals, with my makeup done to perfection, my hair styled in a bubble of soft curls around my pixie face, I don't look my age. As a finishing touch, I stick large silver hoops through the holes in my ears. Maybe one more beer just to get me in the mood.

Before the Legion, Cheryl and I stop at Jibby's Tavern, where I worked from time to time as a bartender, barmaid, dishwasher, salad girl, and second cook. I see a few people I know from the past, but *everyone* knows Cheryl. Drinks appear as if by magic, bought by her friends. I like this girl. She drinks like me, can swear with the best of them, and the drinks are free. I could do this—get back into the single bar scene, have some fun, meet new people, and have a life. As soon as the thought crosses my mind, I feel the familiar weight of guilt settle into my heart. It's how I feel every time I laugh, enjoy a meal, or attempt a new, exciting experience. I know it should have been me that died. I had my chance at a life, and I blew it. Jon paid the price.

Cheryl's gone off to mingle, or something else. It's time for me to leave. I gulp down the rest of my drink, turn on the stool, jump down, and run headlong into a man. "I'm sorry," I mumble, anxious to make my exit.

"I'm not," he replies. "Can I buy you a drink?"

He's attractive, has a nice smile, and is pleasant enough, but the last thing I need is another man in my life. "I've got to go."

"C'mon, one drink, then if you want to leave, I won't argue."

I spy Cheryl. "There's my ride. I should go."

Cheryl isn't ready to leave. She's hooked up with some guy and decides to stay at Jibby's. I have no excuse to refuse the man, who introduces himself as Bill, one drink. Bill orders beer. I order a gin and coke. We talk. We laugh. We flirt. I discover he works for the city in the water department, is divorced, and has one boy who lives with his ex-wife. He is a few years younger than I. I find myself comparing him to Tom. I stop myself short, and ask Bill to drive me home.

———

Windows rolled down in Bill's older pickup truck, we sit in my drive, enjoying the warm summer evening and exchanging bits and pieces about our lives. Bill shares openly. I don't reveal much. If he knows who I've been, it would probably scare him to death. I'm not sure if it is me or the gin talking, but I say, "I read tarot cards." I hadn't touched my cards since some strange events involving them and Jon's death. My skin crawls. I wish I could take the words back.

"Would you read for me sometime?"

"Sure," I say with no intention of doing so. The evening is over for me. I have to get in the house, take a shower, blot the memories from my mind. I am fooling myself if I think I can get back into the dating scene, socialize like nothing happened. "I've got to go." I jump out of the truck.

"Can I call you?"

I turn on the way to the house. "I don't have a phone."

"Can I see you again?"

I shake my head and hurry through the door. What was I thinking? My back against the door, I bury my face in my hands, weep as if it all happened today, and know my life is never going to be any better than it is at this moment.

7

Crazy

"THEY'RE COMIN' TO TAKE ME AWAY, hee hee, ha ha, ho ho," repeats in my mind. I don't know the song, just the one line, but I
can't get it out of my head. I can't stop shaking, rocking, crying.
What am I doing in the middle of the living room floor? Why
can't I get up, pull myself together? I did everything right this
time. How did it go so wrong?

———

There was a man. What was his name? He showed up the last time I spoke with the group about addiction. Another thing that went wrong: the others made it clear they wouldn't be asking me to speak again. It was a cold, wet night in early October, and we'd gone to speak to an Amish community in Tuscola, Illinois. I didn't even know the Amish had problems with alcohol and drugs, but there was a big crowd at the old schoolhouse. I looked out over the audience, many of whom were men with beards and flat black hats, women in long dresses and bonnets, and a number of young people. There was also an older man in the front row that didn't look like he belonged there.

Even though I'd had a few drinks, just to take the chill off and calm my nerves, I wasn't drunk. The group, which consisted of the local sheriff, a doctor, and other concerned professionals, put me in charge of the bong, where they burned pot so the people could identify the odor if they smelled it in their real lives. As I sat there, drawing in great breaths, I began feeling pretty good. I spoke last, but couldn't remember what I said. The crowd filed by to look at the drug paraphernalia, sniff the marijuana. One Amish man, his wife and two teenaged sons in tow, said, "It smells like burning leaves." My response was, "Well, if it's not fall, and you smell that, it's probably pot. That shit just hangs in your buggy." The boys laughed, but their father went to speak to the sheriff who was in charge of the gathering. In the meantime, the out-of-place older gentleman who had looked up at me from the front row walked up, handed me a slip of paper, and said, "In case you ever need us." On it was written "AA," his first name and last initial, and a phone number. Infuriated and insulted, I turned sharply and knocked a glass pipe to the floor, where it shattered into pieces. Who the hell did this guy think he was?

———

What was his name? I need that slip of paper. Drawing in a big gulp of air and releasing it slowly, I struggle to my feet. Rubbing my hands together vigorously, wringing them, I try to stop the shaking to no avail. It's as if I've got one of those diseases, palsy or something. As I rummage through old purses, jackets, it dawns on me: I threw it in a trash can as I left the Amish schoolhouse. Rita! Rita will know his name. Awkwardly, I dial her number. I try to sound casual, and we chat about inane things for seemingly endless minutes. Finally I ask Rita for the man's name. Off the phone, I fumble with the phone book until I find the one she gives me.

Jack C. says, "There's a meeting tonight. Do you think you can stay sober?" No problem, I assure him. An odd calm comes over me. I pour a shot of whiskey, drink it down in one gulp, sit down at the kitchen table, and begin figuring out how I'm going to clean up the mess I've made of everything: my marriage of a few years; my relationship with that husband's kid; my only friend, Cheryl, who that morning told me I had a problem and walked out on me—after some verbal abuse on my part. I can turn things around. I simply have to get a handle on my drinking.

I still don't understand how it all went so wrong, so quickly. After I got out of the nuthouse, I stayed in therapy for years, got my GED, went to college to study psychology, and didn't drink at all. I did smoke some pot and take pills, but certainly not to excess, at least not to my way of thinking. My therapist of many years, who believed alcoholic behavior could be cured through psychotherapy, assured me that I'd know when I could drink like a normal person. I trusted that that day would come.

After nearly eight years of sobriety—during which time I was analyzed, theorized, hypnotized, and graduated from Eastern Illinois University—the day I'd been working toward, waiting for, arrived. The perfect excuse presented itself. In a truck borrowed from Tom, another girl, Nancy, and I made the trip to Bradenton, Florida to retrieve my belongings from my latest failed marriage. I wasn't even 30 years old yet, and my fourth divorce was in process.

I understood why the previous marriages had failed—I'd been drinking. One had taken place in Las Vegas after days of alcohol and speed. I didn't know his last name, but I took it as my own. The other had happened because I got drunk and in an argument with Tom, and he said, "Who would marry you?" I showed him!

But this last one I couldn't figure out. I was stone-cold sober, he swept me off my feet, yet as soon as the "I do's" were exchanged, he changed. It seemed that all those endearing qualities I had, from my outspokenness to my quirky haircut to the way I dressed, along with my kid and dog, were socially unacceptable in his world. Under constant stress, I barely stuck it out for a month.

So it wasn't surprising when, as I sat in a fine seafood restaurant with Nancy on our way to pack up my things from my fourth husband's home, she said, "I think I'll have a glass of wine," and I said, "I think I will too." I'd never been a wine drinker, but damn, it tasted good—like fruit juice with a kick.

———

Now here I am, less than five years later, half drunk, on the verge of a fifth divorce, waiting for a stranger to pick me up to go to an AA meeting. Some days, like today, I think it would be easier to cut my throat and get it over with. I'm tired, so tired, and I wonder if I have enough fight left in me to keep going on. I remember the day Mom killed herself. She said the same thing. I think she was just tired of life, of being unhappy, of not being able to figure it out. Today, I know how she felt. The blare of a car horn brings me out of my reverie. A deep breath, another breath mint, and I'm out the door. What have I got to lose?

After a tense ride, Jack C. turns the car into a parking lot adjacent to a church. "You didn't tell me the meeting is in a church," I say, feeling the anger begin to build. "You didn't ask me," he says, and opens the car door.

I don't do churches. I don't do God. After all, what had he ever done for me except give me pain and misery? "Are you coming?" Jack asks. I shake my head. "Suit yourself," he says, and slams the car door. I watch his back as he walks to the church door and disappears inside.

With the engine shut off, the cold November night begins to creep into my bones. I consider walking uptown to the tavern, but my sweatshirt, vest, and tennis shoes are not suitable for the weather. I can feel my hands shaking. Maybe I'll just go in and warm up a bit.

I hesitate at the church door, but the wintry air drives me inside, down a hallway to a meeting room. Through the door, I hear laughter, smell coffee brewing. A hot cup of coffee would sure taste good right now. I like mine with a shot of whiskey. Probably not going to happen here, I think, and chuckle to myself.

A circle with a triangle in the middle adorns the door. I was right. It's some kind of cult symbol. Torn, but still chilled, I take a deep breath and slip inside the doorway. I'm strong. What can they do to me in an hour? I'll get through it, and I won't come back. It was a stupid idea in the first place. I'm feeling better now, warmer.

Five older men sit at the end of a long table, steaming coffee in white Styrofoam cups and black plastic ashtrays in front of them. "Come in," the white-haired man at the head of the table says. "Coffee's over there." He points. I fight the urge to run, fix a cup of the hot brew with loads of sugar, sit a couple chairs away from the group, and light a cigarette. As they pray and read from a big blue book, my mind wanders to the walls, which are adorned with what look like bumper stickers with sayings on them. Then, I see them: the steps. Twelve steps in bold black letters against a white background. You have got to be kidding. Even if I could, I wouldn't get into that stuff.

Since it's my first meeting, the topic for the evening is the first step: "We admitted we were powerless over our addiction and that our lives had become unmanageable."

I shut out the voices as they share about how they ended up in AA. I don't care. I'm not like these people. I may be an alcoholic, but I can manage my life. I quit before, and I can do it again. I don't need their help. I don't need those ridiculous steps. I certainly don't need some God. Dwight S., the last to speak, looks directly into my eyes and says, "You never have to be alone again." Tears threaten to fall. I push them back. Everyone is looking at me as if expecting me to talk. I shake my head. I'm not telling these people what I did this time to screw up my life.

———

Bill and I didn't date long before he asked me to marry him. It seemed the perfect solution to my problems, my loneliness— especially since I lost Jon. He was fun, liked to party, and didn't mind my drinking, even when I got a bit out of hand. I loved his laid-back attitude, his sense of humor. He could be the one to help me get over my feelings for Tom. This was a golden opportunity—I'd tried everything I could think of to get that man out of my mind. He probably hated me anyway, because of the way I treated him when he came to my door to tell me Jon was dead. I had blamed Tom and said terrible things to him.

Life was good with Bill. He didn't mind me going out with Cheryl, but that was because he didn't know everything we'd been up to. The big trouble began when he got his little boy every other weekend. The first time I looked into the child's eyes, I knew. I saw the hurt, the anger, the helplessness of an abused or neglected child. It touched a place in my heart that I thought I'd completely closed off. It scared me. I wanted to help him, but not get attached to him. I couldn't go through the loss of another child. Every time we had to send him back to his mom and stepdad, it nearly killed me.

I fought for that boy nearly to the point of obsession. I called family services, argued with them, wrote letters to the Illinois state representative, threatened to go to the governor, even called Tom to help us pay for an attorney, all the while continuing to fight forming any emotional attachment with the kid. Bill, on the other hand, didn't seem willing to fight. All of a sudden his laid-back attitude didn't seem so endearing. I didn't understand why he couldn't see the urgency of the situation. I decided if he couldn't stand up for his kid, he would never be able to stand up for me. How could I respect that?

Within the year, Bill and I attained full custody of his son. The boy's mother would have him every other weekend. Every time he left, it made me sick. As hard as I tried not to, I loved that boy. But the truth was, he wasn't my child, and I could only do so much to help him. Unable to cope with my feelings and fears, my drinking escalated. I wasn't a fun drunk anymore—I was angry, even abusive. There were arguments between Bill and me, days of not speaking, until I ended up sitting in the middle of the living room floor in fear of losing my mind.

———

Jack C. pulls his car up in front of my house. He says, "There are meetings somewhere every evening." I nod and get out of the car as quickly as possible. Bill is waiting inside the house, wondering how things went. After I convince him I am not like those AA people, I send him to the liquor store for a bottle. He goes. We drink. The following morning, as I drag myself out of bed, hungover and looking like something the cat dragged in yet again, the terrible truth is reflected in the bathroom mirror.

8

The Cave

NEVER, NOT IN MY WILDEST DREAMS, did I ever imagine I would ever end up here again. I thought I'd lost everything seven years ago—but at least then I had Jon. His indomitable spirit and sense of humor, coupled with the relief over getting away from my fourth husband, made life an adventure. The converted garage that Jon had dubbed "the cave" the first time was the only port we could afford in the raging storm that was our life. It sat back from the street, was surrounded on three sides by trees, and had windows built into the walls that wouldn't open. The tiny apartment's three rooms were separated by peg-board walls. We called the furnishings "shabby chic," but the couch looked like something one would find next to the curb to be picked up by the garbagemen, the mattress on the bed sagged in the middle, and the ancient refrigerator had to be defrosted weekly to keep it from growing icebergs.

We'd lived in dumps many times before, so we knew the drill: bomb for bugs, put boric acid where the floors met the walls and on the outer walls to keep the cockroaches from coming in, scrub with lots of soap and water. I always thought of my mother when we moved into one of those awful places. She would always say, "It's no shame to be poor, but it's a shame to be dirty. Soap's cheap."

———

One hand on the doorknob, I steel myself for the flood of memories when I enter. If I had anywhere else to go, if I could afford something else, I certainly wouldn't be here. But I have to go inside. I'm out of options. The door open, Angel darts past me into the dark interior. I wish I could be more like her—so accepting of whatever situation she's in—and she's been through some harrowing escapades living with me. I used to laugh and say, "If she could talk, I'd have to shoot her." I don't laugh much anymore. Seems like when I do, I get this big knot in my belly and have the urge to vomit.

The past seven years hasn't improved the place. In fact, it's shabbier than when Jon and I lived there. The landlord turned the heat on just enough to warm the living room. When I reach for the knob to turn the heat up, I think of how I used to have to run from the shower in the back of the garage to the front room so I didn't freeze. If I turned the heat up enough to heat the other rooms, it got so hot that Jon couldn't sleep on the couch. I guess I won't have to worry about that anymore.

Perched on the edge of the old brown couch, Angel in my lap, I close my eyes and picture my son, so tall . . . taller than me by the time he turned 13, with thick blond hair that curled around the edges and piercing blue eyes filled with love and trust. We laughed so hard the day I finally found a job. We'd left Florida with nothing but the dog, two suitcases, and very little money. Back in Sullivan, the small town where I'd pissed off so many people and had a well-deserved bad reputation, it was hard to find a job. But I got one washing dishes in a restaurant and lounge. I hated washing dishes—made Jon do them at home—so when I told him, he shot me a smile and said, "Do you think you remember how?"

Dropping Angel, I rush through the bedroom and kitchen to the tiny bathroom. What little I'd eaten that day comes up. I don't know if I'm still having withdrawals from the booze, if it's the ulcers again, or a new wave of guilt and shame caused by having to move back into the garage Jon and I shared as our home for several years. Sometimes I think I should leave Sullivan, but I don't know where I'd go, and I don't have any money. Besides, Jon's buried right outside of town.

The past few weeks have been a living nightmare. I left Bill shortly after he drank with me after that first AA meeting. He believed it when I told him I wasn't like those people at the meeting. He was so sweet and kind, but easily manipulated—not a healthy thing for someone living with me. I told myself I would never be able to live with him and stay sober. The truth was that when things got tough, I got going, one way or another. I'd been running away since the third grade when I discovered Mom's little green-and-white pills.

Christmas had been a bittersweet time. With no place to live, I took a house-sitting job for a few weeks for an older couple who were going back East to spend the holidays with family. The big house, crammed with stuff—the lady hoarded everything from furniture to knickknacks—seemed cold and empty. I figured that if I spent my days cleaning the house, which was no easy chore, it would keep me from thinking about drinking. That worked for a couple of days. The third day, the shakes, vomiting, and insomnia started. The last time I suffered withdrawal, I was shut up in the mental hospital, and the doctors gave me drugs to ease the cravings. I wasn't going back there. With no insurance, I wasn't going to a hospital. I'd screwed up every friendship I had, so there was no one to call . . . that is, no one except those AA people again.

I picked up the phone several times, even dialed a couple of times, only to hang up before anyone answered. Sugar—I needed sugar. Rummaging in the overstocked refrigerator and the stuffed cabinets, I grabbed anything sweet I could find and crammed it into my mouth. I paced, I ate, I threw up, and then I forced myself to eat more. After purging I don't know how many times, I realized the solution to my problem was probably in the medicine cabinet. I jerked it open. Like every other space in the house, it was jam-packed. I started pulling out pill bottles, trying to hold my hands still so I could read them. I finally found some pain pills and dumped them out into my hand, spilling some down the sink. It was the moment of truth.

Still holding the pills in my closed fist, I made the phone call I swore I wouldn't make. I had no idea what I would say if anyone answered. When I heard Jack C.'s deep voice, all I could do was weep, sobbing into the receiver. Patiently, he waited until I could squeak out a few words, and said, "Well, why don't you come over here?" He only lived a few blocks away. Fumbling with buttons and zipper, I bundled up and trudged through the snow—because between the shakes and stomach cramps, I knew I couldn't drive.

Unaware until I arrived at the house that it was Christmas Eve, it struck me as strange that Jack had told me to come over when he obviously had company. I hesitated at the end of the driveway full of cars and stared at the house, decorated in blinking lights with a wreath on the door. When I would have turned to leave, the door opened. Jack motioned me inside. His four grown boys were there, three of whom I discovered were also in AA. One by one, they left the room until I was alone at the kitchen table with Jack and a half a cup of coffee that I could barely get to my mouth without sloshing all over myself and the table.

My arms crossed, hands tucked under each armpit to keep them from shaking, I stood and paced back and forth as I poured out my pain to this virtual stranger. He listened. He waited. When I'd exhausted myself, he shared with me some of his story, including how he got through withdrawal. Then he said, "It's not forever. This too shall pass." "When?" my mind screamed. Jack didn't seem to notice. He smiled, rose, reached up to a shelf and pulled down a box, which he handed to me. It was tea. For God's sake . . . tea? How was tea going to help?

Jack drove me home as I clutched the bag of items he called the withdrawal emergency kit. The last thing he said to me was, "If you think you're going to drink or drug, call me first." I nodded. Inside, I unloaded the items and stood staring at them. I didn't believe herbal tea, honey, Epsom salts, and hard candy would help, but it was worth a try. If all else failed, then I'd consider the pills.

Purposefully, I set forth the plan Jack had laid out for me. In the bathroom, I lit some candles I found in a drawer, placed them around the tub filled with hot water, bubble bath, and Epsom salts, stuck a chunk of strawberry candy in my mouth, and lowered my ravaged body slowly into the water. It felt like heaven. It was the best I'd felt in days. Staring into the flickering flame of a candle, I began to question the choices I'd made that brought me to that moment in time. Tears welled up in my eyes. I let my body slide beneath the water. Why couldn't I just let go . . . end it all? Running out of air, I popped up quickly, drew in a deep breath, and considered what was going to happen to me. What would I do when the owners of the house came home? Then I remembered something Jack told me. He said, "Don't worry about tomorrow, or the next hour, even the next moment. All the worry in the world won't change one thing. All you have to concentrate on is the moment and not putting anything nasty in your mouth."

It was a long night filled with hot baths, herbal tea loaded with sugar and honey, and candy, but finally I slept. It was a deep sleep, the sleep only those exhausted with life can understand. By morning, I did feel better, but I looked like hell. Jack invited me over for breakfast and to spend Christmas day with him and his family. It was time for some damage control. I did the best I could with what clothes and makeup I'd brought with me and made my way to Jack's house, even though everything in me told me to turn on my heel and run away. The truth was, I'd run out of anyplace to run. If I didn't like it there, I could always say I was sick and leave.

As soon as the door opened, I felt the warmth from the kitchen, smelled bacon cooking, and wondered if I would be able to eat. Jack and his boys were busy cooking, setting the table, and talking to each other. They seemed so normal that it was hard for me to fathom any of them ever being an alcoholic . . . being like me. They welcomed me, ushered me to the table, and set a plate in front of me. Jack fixed me a cup of tea, the same stuff I'd been drinking all night, and some toast with butter and jelly. I picked at it, eating slowly, ever mindful that it might not stay down.

After breakfast, we retired to the living room. I wanted to light a cigarette, but hesitated until I saw one of the boys pull a pack out of his pocket. I began to relax a bit. To my horror, one of the boys said they were going to open presents. Talk about feeling out of place! I got up to leave. Jack insisted that I stay. He handed out gifts, and to my amazement there were some for me. I didn't know what to think, do, or say. I couldn't imagine where or when they had gotten the gifts, but the gesture touched my heart in a very special way. As I tore the paper away, I didn't even care what was inside—just that people I hardly knew had gone out of their way for me.

———

The money I make for house-sitting and cleaning pays the rent for the converted garage, but soon I will have to find work or be hungry and homeless. I've been both from time to time and know how to survive on very little—but I've had to do some pretty disgusting things sometimes for money. No way could I do those things sober.

I can't sit here in this filthy apartment all day. Unloading the car will have to wait until the place is clean. Thank God the shakes and vomiting have stopped. I still don't sleep much, and the alcoholic itch nearly drives me crazy at times—it feels like I have crabs all over my body. Jack says it's because my nerves are coming back to life. As I scrub the toilet, I think of all the old, filthy toilets I've cleaned, both mine and those of others. I wonder if there will ever be a time when I'll live in a nice house with new stuff that really looks clean after I work so hard. Finished, the toilet as good as I can get it, I sit at the kitchen table, pull a pouch of tobacco and papers from my purse, and roll a cigarette.

It reminds me of sitting in my first husband Jim's dad's room so many years ago. I'm not much better off than he was. It doesn't matter, though. This is my life, and it will probably not get any better. One cave or another . . . it makes no difference.

9

Broke

AT THE TINY WOODEN KITCHEN TABLE that I've shoved in one corner so I have room to cook, I pull out the candy tin in which I keep the cigarette butts I steal from ashtrays outside public buildings and strike a match. It's a wonder I haven't got hoof-and-mouth disease or something else, smoking other people's butts. I push the thought from my mind, draw in the hot smoke, and let it out slowly. I'm going to have to make another butt run again soon. I almost got caught the last time in front of the grocery store. A woman walked up, and I acted like I was putting my cigarette out. I still wonder if she knew.

As much as I hated living in cities, sometimes I yearn for the anonymity of them, for a place where no one knows me, where I don't have to deal with the stares, the whispered comments, the people in the nicer stores watching me like I'm going to steal something. Looking at the small amount of cash in front of me, the realization of how dire my circumstances have become hits me. I've got to get a job. I know I could go back to working in the bars, but I also know I'll drink again if I do. I talked about it in the meeting tonight. The only advice they had for me was to pray about it. Are they insane? That's the dumbest thing I ever heard. If there is a God, why would he give a damn where I work?

Two weeks. I've got enough money to last two more weeks; then I don't know what I'll do. I could call Tom. He would help me; he always helped me. No! The price is too high. I've got to do this myself. God, I need a drink. Will I ever not need a drink? I envy those people at the meetings who say the desire to drink has been lifted from them. I think about alcohol every day, fight the urge, and attend meetings each night so I won't end up in a bar. Yet instead of getting easier, it's getting harder.

Jack and some other ex-drunks took me to a speaker meeting the other night. Neva G., whom I'd met before and thought was nothing more than a dried-up old windbag, told her story. She'd been sober over twenty-five years. Her words struck a note in my heart. It took everything in me to hold back tears, partly because of her story and partly because of my shame for some of the things I'd said and thought about her. I remember saying to one girl, "Jesus Christ, what did she do . . . jump off the Ark and start a meeting?" We laughed. That night, the words came back to choke me.

Neva smiled coolly as I approached. I hadn't been very nice to her, but I needed her help; I needed to know how she finally got over the constant urge to drink. I put my hand out. She shook it. I asked the question on my mind. "How?" She studied my face for what seemed like long moments, and said, "I turned my will and life over to a God of my understanding each morning, and it finally left me." I don't know if I rolled my eyes, or if the expression on my face told my attitude about that particular step, but she said, "Do you pray?" I didn't respond. She said, "Do you know any prayers?"

Each meeting began with the Serenity Prayer and closed with the Lord's Prayer. I never said them, had never memorized them, and had no intention of doing so, but I nodded. The only prayer I knew by heart was a child's prayer, and I don't even know where I learned it. You can bet it wasn't at my parents' house. It played through my mind: "Now I lay me down to sleep. I pray the Lord my soul to keep. If I die before I wake, I pray the Lord my soul to take." I wasn't about to admit to this woman that at age 35, that was really the only prayer I knew.

Neva said, "How your sobriety goes, and for that matter how your life in sobriety goes, will be contingent on your spiritual condition. You know, you don't even have to believe. You just have to try it. I began by reading three prayers out loud each morning." I must have looked skeptical, because when she continued, she said, "You know, Barb, you will experiment with insanity and death before you will experiment with spirituality," and she turned to leave.

——

A low growl from Angel tells me it's time to fix something to eat. It will be dried soup and crackers again. After pouring hot water into the Styrofoam container, I wait three minutes, dip out most of the noodle soup into a bowl, add crackers to the remaining broth, stir it until it cools, and pour it into the dog dish. It's a good thing she's so small or I wouldn't be able to feed her. Neva's words haunt me as I eat. Is she right? Should I give prayer a try? What's the worst thing that could happen?

Immediately, past prayers, unheard prayers, prayers that never worked, memories of my dead kids, my mother, even my childhood dog, Pedro, make me question what she said. My second thought is simply, what else do I have to lose? The only thing I have left that I really care about is my old dog. Before I clear the table, I look up at the white ceiling tiles and say, "Okay God, if you're up there, if you put a job in front of me, any job, I'll take it." Now, we'll see what happens.

To clear my mind, I strip off my clothes and step into the miniscule bathroom off the kitchen for a shower. I wish I had a bathtub so I could soak in some Epsom salts and bubble bath like I did when I was at that house at Christmas. No matter; even if I had a tub, I couldn't afford the Epsom salts or bubble bath.

With no television or radio and major insomnia, the nights are long. My landlady had a rummage sale last week, and I spotted a box filled with ballpoint paints, barely used, and a quilt ring. I bought the whole box and a white sheet for three dollars. Carefully, I cut the sheet into squares, drew pictures on them, and now I'm painting them. Jack said I needed to get a hobby. It keeps me from thinking about drinking. If I ever get all the squares done, I'll sew them together and call it my sober quilt . . . that is, assuming I'm still sober.

———

Angel is my alarm clock. At six o'clock every morning she's up and ready to be let out. It doesn't seem to matter to her that I didn't doze off until the middle of the night. It's a good thing this morning, because I'm supposed to meet Jack for breakfast, and it will be another long day of looking for a job. The job prayer flashes through my mind. I laugh it off, throw on some clothes, feed the dog, and trudge through snow the two blocks to the local coffee shop. I can barely wait for a steaming cup of coffee. One of the things I'll buy when I get a job is a coffeepot.

The aroma of fried bacon, eggs, and warm bread embraces me as I step into the cozy cafe, stomp the snow off my boots, and hang my coat on the wooden hall tree by the door. Several people whom I know from the meetings smile and wave. I spot Jack, who is sitting with a man I'm not familiar with, near the back of the room. He's probably another ex-drunk. I can't believe how many of them there are in such a small town. I can't wait to sit down. Jack's going to buy breakfast. Thank God, or it would be a long, hungry day.

Jack introduces the man as Dan, we order, and begin to chat. When Jack asks if I'm going to look for work today, the man says, "Are you looking for a job?" The hairs on the back of my neck stand up. "I know a woman," he continues, "that might be looking for someone to help with her mother. You should give her a call." He scribbles a name and phone number on a napkin and hands it to me. Before I can respond, the food arrives. It's not something I would choose to do, but the thought of making money, of what I could buy if I had a job, drives me to ask the cafe owner if I can use the phone after breakfast. She's been great about letting me give her phone number out when looking for work, since I don't have a phone at home.

My heart pounds as I punch in the numbers. I really need this job. A woman answers. I ask about the situation. She says she doesn't need anyone at the moment, but she'll take my name and number. I hang up, knowing she'll never call. No one is ever going to call. I sowed my wild drunken oats all over town, did disgusting things, left a man whom everyone thinks of highly—why would anyone want to hire me . . . except the bars, for obvious reasons? Defeated, I drag myself home, put on my old robe, crawl under a blanket on the couch with Angel, and cry until I fall asleep.

For three days, I hole up in the garage, only getting dressed in time for meetings. At the meetings, I try to shut out the voices of those whose lives are getting better. I just can't listen to any more candy-coated stories about how much better their lives are . . . who cares? My life is shit. I begin to question why I'm even here, why I'm sober, why I don't go get a job at one of the bars and drink until I die. Who would really care? I tried to talk to Jack about how I've been feeling. He suggested I go get a physical. A physical? I can't afford to take Angel to the vet, let alone a doctor who would give me a prescription I can't pay for.

The morning of the fourth day, I awaken resolved about my circumstances. I'm out of options. I don't care what those AA people say about working around booze. They aren't going to support me. I'm going to march into that cafe this morning and tell Jack my decision. It's my life. I have to do what I have to do to survive. I tried it their way, and it isn't working.

Since I'm going to apply for a job this morning, I take extra care with my hair and makeup, dress in my better clothes, and drive to the restaurant. I hate to use the gas, but it's too far and too cold to walk. Steeling myself for the disappointed look on Jack's face when I tell him what I'm going to do, I jerk the door open. Before I have time to remove my coat, the owner steps up to me, digs in her apron pocket, and hands me a slip of paper. "You're supposed to call this woman," she says. I look at the number. It's unfamiliar. Maybe it's the nursing home, or the kitchen job at the school, or it could be the office at the refuse place. "You can use the phone if you want," the owner says.

I make the call. It's the woman who's been looking for a health-care person for her mother . . . the one Dan told me about. Could I come and meet her and her mother today . . . in an hour? It will be a temporary position until her regular health-care worker gets back on her feet from a medical problem. Could I? I can barely contain myself.

"I think I got a job," I say when I join Jack at the table. He buys breakfast to celebrate. I ask if he knows anything about the family. He says they are good people, active in the church, and the mother used to own one of those really nice dress shops up on the square—the same square where I used to drink. My heart sinks. My breakfast becomes tasteless. What if they know who I am, the things I've done? What will I tell them about myself? I have to tell them something. I'm sure if I don't, someone in that little town would be happy to inform them. I have to go. I'll simply tell them whatever they ask of me truthfully, and hope for the best.

On the way to the house, I remember the prayer. Was it possible those people in the meeting knew what they were talking about? It doesn't matter. I probably won't get the job anyway. Some of Jack's wisdom slips into my mind. He told me once that if I think something will be dreadful, it will be; with my attitude, I'll make it happen. Parked in front of the house, I take several deep breaths, let them out slowly, put a smile on my face, and get out of the car. I'm going to get this job if I have to beg for it.

A couple of hours later, I'm flying high. I got the job. I don't know if it's because they really liked me, or because they are desperate for help and need it right away . . . but I got the job. They were so nice. I told them the truth, told them I go to meetings at night, that I am trying to get my life turned around—and they hired me anyway. Helen, the woman with Parkinson's whom I will be caring for, and I clicked right off the bat. I can do this. I make a promise to myself on the way home. I won't steal anything. I won't drink alcohol. And, I will take the best care of the lady that I am able to give. I can't wait to get home to tell Angel, to go to my meeting tonight with some good news.

The prayer enters my mind. I push it away and think of the things I can buy with my first paycheck: cigarettes, real dog food, maybe that coffeepot. Finally, a ray of hope in my dark world.

10

The Dress

DWIGHT S., A SMALL-STATURED WHITE-HAIRED MAN originally from Kentucky and chairman of tonight's meeting, says, "Is anyone celebrating a birthday?" All heads turn toward me.

I raise my hand and say, "Hi, I'm Barb, and I'm an alcoholic, and I've got one year." Among accolades for my great achievement, I get a hug and my hard-won metal chip from Dwight. The previous chips, for three months, six months, and nine months, are colorful cheap plastic, but they go all out for year-birthdays. After what they did for my six-month birthday, I'm a bit nervous about what they have in mind now.

By the time I had six consecutive months of sobriety, I'd pretty much settled into my life. Helen and I had formed a wonderful bond, and I was her permanent day caregiver, which left evenings free for me to attend meetings. The five older men from my local meeting on Monday nights, along with Helen and her family, were my friends—although I still spent time with Cheryl occasionally. The relationship changed after I got sober, and I envied her because she could still run the bars, drink, and go dancing. I cringed inside when she shared stories about the people she partied with, but said nothing. The party was over for me.

Since Angel and I lived a pretty quiet life, I'd been able to pay off some bills and finally got a phone, which turned out to be both a blessing and a curse. Tom began calling, sometimes sober, sometimes drunk. Mostly, I hung up on him. In fact, after a while, when he did call the first thing he would say is, "Don't hang up . . . don't hang up." Seeing him was not an option, because I knew it would weaken my resolve. All I had to do was think about looking into those pale blue eyes. My stomach instantly got butterflies, and my heart beat faster. I still thought of him every morning when I got up and every night when I retired. But, as much as I'd admitted to myself I was in love with him, that he was the only man I'd ever truly loved, I knew it was never going to happen for us.

I immersed myself in meetings every night, my work with Helen, and painting my sober quilt. As much as I enjoyed going to the meetings in surrounding towns, my favorite remained my local meeting where it had been just me and the five older men. I felt safe and comfortable there. I liked being the only woman. I'd never been at ease with other women. I drank like a man, worked like a man, and could swear like a truck driver. Which explains my shock when I received my six-month gift from the men in my group.

————

Jack said, "There's a women's luncheon in Champaign next month." Before I could respond, he said, "We got you a ticket." My mind denied what he'd said, but I smiled and accepted the ticket. There had to be a way to get out of it gracefully; I didn't want to hurt their feelings. They were beaming as if they'd given me something I really wanted. Maybe I could lose the ticket. No, they'd buy me another one. I couldn't be obvious.

As the time for the luncheon grew closer, I put my next plan into action. I said, "I don't think I can go. My old car isn't running that well. I'd be afraid to drive it out of town." In short order, they found me a ride with a woman I could barely tolerate in a meeting. Two hours trapped in a car with her would surely drive me to drink. Again, I smiled and nodded.

A few days later, about to panic, I said, "I don't think I can go. I don't have a dress, and I can't afford to buy one. I know I'll feel out of place if I have to wear jeans." A huge mistake! A few days later, they presented me with a dress. They borrowed one from Susan F., who to my way of thinking was the worst-dressed woman in AA. It sported huge colorful flowers, green leaves, and since she towered over me by several inches, the length was unflattering. It was god-awful. At the thought of wearing it I nearly threw up.

The reason I didn't wear dresses, at least according to the therapist I had seen after being released from the mental hospital, was that when I put on a dress and high heels, I felt like a hooker. The problem stemmed from a really tough time in my life when I had had to dress up to entice men and got paid for sex. Of course there wasn't much chance of enticing any man in the borrowed dress. But, still, the feeling remained. The only thing left was to get sick. I'd wait until a couple of days passed before I dropped the bomb.

On the Friday before the Sunday luncheon Jack picked me up for the meeting. The time had come to put my plan into action. Before I told him I thought I might be coming down with something, he handed me a box. A corsage—they'd bought me a corsage to match the dress. I knew they wanted me to feel special. At that moment, if my heart hadn't swollen with love for those men, I would have told him I had syphilis if I thought it would get me out of going. But I was doomed.

I couldn't sleep the night before. What in the world do a room full of women do without men? What would I talk about? How could I wear that dress out in public? Questions whirled through my mind all night. By morning, not only did the dress look bad—I looked like the last rose of summer. I don't even know why I bothered with hair and makeup, because all anyone would see coming was the huge flower garden I had on.

At 8:30 A.M., my driver waited on the street in front of the garage apartment. I rushed out in the hope that no one I knew would see me. When I jumped in the car, the driver looked askance and sharply turned her head back to the road ahead. I caught the look, thought about explaining my attire, and then decided I didn't care. It was a one-time thing. I'd get through it. I probably wouldn't know anyone there anyway. And who cared what this woman thought, or any of the others. I just wanted to get it over with.

The woman prattled on for the first hour of the drive about her children, their kids, lives, and the problems she had with them. Tired, so tired of listening to her, I said, "Well, at least your kids are alive." That stopped the conversation. My head pressed against the glass, I dozed. The next thing I knew, we were pulling into a parking lot in front of a hotel with a big, fancy restaurant. Other women dressed in expensive-looking summer suits and dresses, some with colorful silk scarves thrown casually around their necks and coiffed hairdos, filed into the entrance. My heart sank. Everything in me shouted to get out of the car and run away. There was nowhere to run. If at that moment I'd had a bottle in my purse, I would have drunk it down. Hell, most of my life I'd had to drink to get ready to go out to drink.

Bolstering what courage I had, I walked in behind my driver, hurriedly gave the woman at a table near the door my ticket, and rushed past groups of women chatting in the foyer to find my seat. As difficult as it would be to blend in, I wanted to give it a try. At least at the table they could only see the top half of me.

But that didn't last long. As soon as the meeting started, they called for a sobriety countdown. They began with one day of sobriety. One woman stood. She looked better than I did. A hot flash began at the top of my head and moved down my body. Sweat trickled down my back. When they called six months, could I stand in all my glory? Dark rings under my arms completed my ensemble from Hell. The chairwoman called out, "six months."

I hesitated, then stood. Piss on them. I'd worked my ass off for those months. After the applause, I returned to my seat, and the woman next to me said, "Way to go," and patted my arm. Next, she said, "It took me nearly four years to get my first year." I began to relax.

In spite of the dress, it turned out to be a wonderful experience. I listened to the women speakers, one from AA and one from Al-Anon, realized they didn't always look the way they did at that moment, that they'd acted atrociously too, and shared stories with the women from my table outside over a cigarette. It had been a long time since I laughed so much.

———

Now I've been sober for a year, and the time has come. Some of the members are taking me out for a sandwich after the meeting. As much as I enjoyed my six-month excursion, the time leading up to it, the ride to Champaign, and my imagination just about did me in. What's up now?

Jack, myself, and several others settle around a semi-circlular table in the local fast-food restaurant before Jack says, "The Illinois State Convention is going to be in Decatur this year. Barb and I are going to be on the planning committee." I elbow the woman next to me, and whisper, "Do I have to wear a dress?" She laughs, "No, it's pretty casual."

"And," Jack continues, "Barb is going to be our speaker at the end of the month."

I can't do that. I won't do it. He can't make me do it, I think. Yet somewhere in the deepest part of me, I know I'll do it. I want to be sober. I want to sit among these people, to continue to know a sense of belonging that I've never known before. I picture the sign inside the meeting room that says WELCOME HOME. That's what it's like for me. It's that place where I'm not judged, where people understand because they've been where I've been, where they don't want anything from me except to help me find a better way of life. Yes, I'll do it if that's what it takes. If I could get through going out in public in that horrible dress, I could do about anything.

11

Do or Drink

TODAY IS SUNDAY. I awaken with that old familiar feeling of dread. I know it's partly because Helen is in the hospital with a blood disorder, which has brought home the reality that she won't be with me much longer. It's not about the money—although my finances are always a concern—but I love her. As much as I told myself I would never allow myself to have deep feelings for another human being again, to risk the pain of loss, I couldn't help it. She is the epitome of the way people are supposed to be: kind, loving, giving, generous, and nonjudgmental. However, there is something else going on I can't quite put my finger on.

Normally I would be up early, getting ready to be picked up for the 8:00 A.M. Sunday morning meeting in Mattoon. This Sunday I can linger over coffee and a smoke. I'm going to attend a brunch and speaker meeting in Decatur with Jack and several other members of AA. I was thrilled to be invited, but the more I think about it and try to figure out something appropriate to wear from my limited wardrobe, the less excited I am. I sure didn't mention wardrobe at the meeting last night, especially after the flowered dress fiasco over a year ago.

Dressed in a gray sweat suit, Angel in her sweater and hooked to the leash, we begin our usual trek several blocks to the local park. My thoughts wander over the past year as Angel stops here and there to take in some new, exciting smells. My days have been filled with taking care of Helen, although, at least emotionally, I think she takes care of me. Bit by bit, I've shared my story with her, have told her things I've never revealed in AA meetings. We've laughed together, cried together, and I trust her counsel above that of all others.

A few months ago, the men in my local meeting insisted it was time for me to get a woman sponsor. They had a woman in mind. I contacted her, met with her, and we'd been meeting regularly ever since. One day, I tried to talk to her about Tom, who still called frequently. Before I could explain that I'd been in love with him since the age of 20, that I had thought of him every morning, every evening, all those years, and that I still do, she shut me down. She might as well have been standing on a chair, wagging her finger at me while she told me that I was not ready for a relationship, that I needed to stay away from him, that all I needed to be concerned about was my sobriety and accepting my life as is. I wanted to tell her that I needed to resolve the situation with Tom, deal with my feelings, so that I might find a bit of peace in my sobriety, but I realized it would be an exercise in frustration.

The following day, I approached Helen, whom I'd spoken to many times about Tom. She said, "Do you love him?" I nodded, barely able to contain the flood of tears that threatened to fall. She was thoughtful for a moment before she said, "Maybe you ought to open the lines of communication instead of hanging up on him every time he calls. Keep the door open. You never know what might happen."

A sob escaped from the deepest part of me. I wept. What Helen suggested was what I wanted, but fear held me back. Tom was the one person with the capability of hurting me beyond repair. Helen pulled the bedcover back and said, "When you stop taking risks in life, you might as well crawl in here with me."

The next time Tom rang, I took Helen's advice. I felt like a teenager with a new boyfriend, right down to the fluttering heart and butterflies. I let him in.

Then, it happened. He showed up in Sullivan late one night and called me. He was drunk and told me that the police said if he didn't get off the square they were going to arrest him. Against my better judgment, I drove to the square and let Tom follow me home, my only intention being to get him sobered up so he could drive back to Mattoon. But he wanted to stay at my place. I refused. He said he didn't have enough gas to get home. I told him I'd follow him to the gas station. He said he was too tired to drive. I told him I'd get him a room at the motel. He tried every ploy he could think of before he finally gave up and left.

I had taken the risk. It didn't work out, but it didn't kill me. I still loved him, would probably love him until the day I died, but that didn't mean I could be with him. I learned a valuable lesson that night. I'd walked through a fear that had haunted me for years. I accepted the truth of my feelings for Tom, but understood that it was time to tuck them away and never drag another man, like all my ex-husbands whom I didn't love, into my life. If I couldn't be with Tom, it was time to live my life as a single, independent woman . . . sober.

———

By the time Angel and I arrive back at the apartment, I'm feeling better. It's time to get showered and dressed for the day ahead. Having remembered the risk I took with Tom, I can put on a brave face and get through a new experience today. I don't know why everything new I do has to be a struggle, but maybe one day, if I keep trying, facing my fears, it will get better. Something Jack told me early in my sobriety crosses my mind. He said, "From this moment on, you don't owe anyone anything anymore." It seems like all my life I'd done things I didn't want to do for people I didn't particularly like for one reason or another, but usually to make them like me or to feel as if I fit in. Maybe that's where my current feeling of dread is coming from—worrying about fitting in today.

My ride is here. I scoot into the backseat next to Anne and Patty, both dressed in nice dresses and heels. Jack turns from the driver's seat and comments on how attractive I look. I assure myself I look presentable in the beige slacks and a crisp white cotton blouse I picked up at a thrift store. I spent a lot of time washing them out by hand. I hung them near the heater to dry, then pressed them on a towel on the kitchen table.

By the time we reach the Holiday Inn in Decatur, I am relaxed. We've been sharing drinking stories, talking about different meetings, and I forget to worry about what I'm wearing. It's going to be a good day. Inside, we're ushered to a table for six where Paul, a longtime friend of Jack, awaits our arrival.

The problems begin with a tray of six champagne flutes on the waiter's tray. It's a champagne brunch! For every patron who is buying a meal, the golden bubbly is free. The others laugh and decline the wine, but I want it, can't take my eyes off the chilled, sweating glasses, can almost taste it, feel the oblivion take hold. It takes everything in me not to tackle the waiter as he walks away, grab the glasses, and drink every drop.

On the way home, I feel like I've been in a blackout for the past three hours. I know I was there, ate the meal, listened to the speakers, and met new people, but it's all a blurry background behind the tray of drinks foremost in my thoughts. When the car pulls in front of the apartment, I can't get out, away from the others, fast enough. I've had an epiphany. Either I'm an absolute fraud, or there is something seriously wrong with me.

As soon as the car turns the corner, I gather up Angel, jump in my own car, and drive to the cemetery. It's not unusual to visit the graveside of my son on the weekends, to sit near his gravestone and talk to him about my week, the changes in my life. This day, it's different. I can't stop crying, don't feel the connection to him, my thoughts consumed with the times I sat in that very spot and drank whiskey until the gut-wrenching pain in my heart was obliterated. I don't know what to do with that pain anymore. It's like an open wound with no salve.

Exhausted, cried out, I drag myself back to the car. Upon leaving, I turn the opposite way out of the cemetery drive, take the road through Kirkland to the highway so I don't have to pass the liquor store on my way into town. I barely got past it on the way out of town. At home, I pace back and forth through the three rooms, my mind working furiously. Is everybody else in the program doing what I've realized I'm doing—mouthing the prayers and slogans, going with the flow, all the while wondering why I'm doing it this time? Am I simply working another system to meet some sick need to belong? Am I deluding myself into believing I can ever be any better than I've ever been? What is the point of it all? The kids are dead, the husbands and boyfriends gone. I basically have no family left that wants anything to do with me, and my life is going nowhere.

I'm so tired. I drop onto my bed and pull the blanket up to my neck. What I wouldn't give to go to sleep and never wake up. The prayer crosses my mind. I say, "If I die before I wake, I pray the Lord, my soul to take." Maybe I'll be reunited with my kids, Mom, and my Aunt Ruthie. Angel jumps on the bed to curl up next to me. What would happen to her if I died? What about Helen? Helen needs me. She would be so disappointed if she could see me now. Once she told me she loved me so much that if I ever took another drink, she would fire me.

For a moment, thinking of Helen calms me. But she's dying, has told me she is ready to go at any time. Her undying faith allows her to believe a part of her will go on, will be reunited with her loved ones. I want to believe that. but I don't. All I can think of is the pain I'll suffer when she leaves me. As much as I appreciate the meetings, Helen and Angel keep me from crossing that fine line back to insanity.

What a time we've had together. I love being at Helen's house, fixing her meals, having someone to eat with and talk to. She lets me bring Angel to work with me because my apartment is so hot in the summer. I stay cool at night by soaking a sheet in cool water and laying it on the floor, where I can sleep in front of a fan. Helen's nicely furnished, air-conditioned house is a blessing. One of the few things Helen can still enjoy is food. We come up with all kinds of ideas for special meals. On her birthday, I surprised her. She loves to read Essie Sommers romance novels, which are set in England. I'm hooked on them too. In the back of some of the books are recipes for English food. Using the recipes, I created her an entire English meal, from Scotch eggs to Yorkshire pudding. Some of it was edible, some of it not so much. We ate. We laughed. We decided English cooking was not my forte.

Although the family is paying me as if I'm working, I can't wait for Helen to get home from the hospital so we can get back to our normal routine. I suppose I should call one of those AA people. That's what they tell us to do when we are in crisis. It's hard, when I have this much time sober, to admit the truth. Today, I want to drink more than I want to be sober. I tell myself I can't listen to any more AA crap. I resent those I go to with my problems who quote the book, bring up the steps, and tell me to pray. I'm doing the best I can. As soon as I think it, I know it's a lie.

Other members of AA have made suggestions. I've tried some of them. I have three prayers taped to my bathroom mirror. I read them out loud each morning, but they are meaningless words. I try praying, to make an effort each night to write down three things for which I'm thankful. I've started half-assed attempts at making amends to those I've hurt. It all seems like just another con on my part. I don't mean it. I don't feel resolved. It's those damn steps and the God stuff that are holding me back. Maybe I'm like one of those people mentioned in the big book who are constitutionally incapable of being honest with themselves.

I won't get drunk today. I want to be there for Helen when she comes home. Reluctantly, I pick up the phone and punch in the numbers.

12

Awakening

IT'S NEARLY EASTER. Carefully threading the needle, I tie it off
in a knot and push it through the thick white fur. Another few
days, and I'll be finished with the Easter rabbit costume I'm
making for the big egg hunt at the park. It has been a job sewing the entire thing by hand, but the extra money will come
in handy. I'm saving up for a small window air conditioner to
buy before the sweltering days of summer hit. The landlord said
they would remove a window so I could have it installed if I
agree to leave it there if I move. Since I don't know how I'll

ever have enough money to move, I agree to the terms. I can't go through another summer like last year.

No one could have been any happier than I to see the new grass sprouting through the soil, trees budding, and flower shoots poking their heads up to meet the sun. It was a tough winter. On the coldest nights, Angel and I curled up on the old couch together and shared body heat. Every two to four hours the alarm sounded, informing me I had to get up to start the car, let it run for a few minutes, and place a heavy rug over the radiator. If I didn't, it would be frozen up in the morning, and I'd have to walk to work.

Before someone told me how to keep my car going, I walked a lot. When the temperature dropped drastically, I went to my meeting and shared my plight with the local men. I thought surely one of them would start giving me a ride or at least look at the car. It's not like I could afford to take it to a garage. Instead, one of them said, "Do you have good boots?" I did. He said I should be grateful for that, and put an end to the conversation. I seethed throughout the hour meeting, stomped home through the snow and ice, took the boots off, and threw them against the wall of the tiny living room.

Early the following morning, the same man showed up at my apartment, put jumpers on my battery, got the car started, and told me how to keep it going in the frigid weather. I regretted the horrible names I had called him in the privacy of my home the night before. The truth was that he was right to ask about the boots. I hadn't always had them. Years ago, when I attended college at Eastern Illinois University in Charleston and lived on state aid, Jon, Angel, and I lived in a tiny motel room that had been converted into an efficiency apartment. The only pair of shoes I had gave out, the soles separating from the leather. I had to go to class. With only a few dollars to my name, I ran into one of those dollar stores. There was a basket of sandals on sale. I grabbed a pair, paid for them, and left. I didn't realize until I got to school and put them on that they were two entirely different shoes. I had to wear them.

The final stitches in the big rabbit feet done, I stuff the ends with cotton wadding and go to check on the papier-mâché head. Once it dries, I will add another layer of newspaper soaked in the flour, salt, and water mixture. I love making costumes and have been making them since Jon started school. At Halloween when he was in the first grade, I made him an entire knight costume from cardboard, tinfoil, and glue. He won first place. After that, people began asking me to make costumes for them. It has always been a good source of extra income.

Easter Sunday I awaken to a strange sound. Opening the door to let Angel out, I can't believe my eyes. Everything is covered in ice, the trees and power lines sagging from the weight of it, blades of grass and flowers frozen in mid-growth, the car completely covered with a layer of ice. I won't be going anywhere today . . . and what about my rabbit? Although I feel bad for the kids who won't be at the park for the Easter egg hunt, I'm glad I already got paid for the costume.

Between the money I made for the costume and money I made at Christmas for creating handmade piñatas, I have enough stuck away in a can in the kitchen cabinet to purchase the air conditioner. Things are looking better.

Spring comes slowly, but with the bright sunshine emerges a feeling of hope. I don't mind the cold, or the snow and ice, but I hate the gray days that seem to last forever in Illinois. One more week, and I'll be going to the store to buy a small air conditioner for my bedroom. It will be like heaven after last year. I'm proud that for the first time in my life, I'm doing things right: working, paying my own bills, making my way in life without the help of a man, without lying or cheating anyone. It feels good.

———

Something is wrong with Angel. I fall to the floor next to her jerking body. She goes limp in my arms. NO! Not my Angel. God, please don't take her from me. I can't breathe. I can't think. I've got to do something. Laying her gently on the bed, I dial Jack's number. He comes quickly. By the time he arrives, Angel is up, but disoriented and walking in circles. Carefully, I wrap her in a blanket and hold her close as Jack drives us to the vet.

"It sounds like a seizure," the vet says. "I'll have to run some tests."

An hour later, I'm home alone. I didn't want to leave her, but had no choice. I pace. I want to pray, but the words won't come. When I asked God to take care of my son, he died. I can't lose Angel. She's all I have. Startled by the ring of the phone, I run to grab the receiver and answer. It's the vet. He wants to see me. "Is she okay?," I say, unsure if I want to hear the answer. He assures me she will be all right, but he needs to talk to me about her condition. She has epilepsy.

On the drive to the vet's office, I consider what I know about epilepsy. One of Dad's wives had it. Once, she fell on the floor against a heat vent, and it left terrible burns on her body. I look at the can on the seat next to me. I wonder if I'll have enough money to pay for the tests. I can live without the air conditioner, but I'm not sure I can make it without Angel.

Inside, I can't believe she looks so good. She seems like her old self, licking, wagging her tail, so happy to see me. I'm relieved. The vet says, "You've got some decisions to make. She's going to have this for the rest of her life. There is medication you can give her to control the seizures, but at her age. . . ." He gives me a look. I know what he's talking about. It's not going to happen. I'll do whatever I have to, but he's not killing my dog.

Back home, lying across the bed with Angel next to me, I look into her large, brown, trusting eyes and say, "No matter what, I'll always take care of you. No one will ever hurt you." I can't hold back the tears. Helen's going to die. Angel's going to die. Life is never going to get any better. I need a drink. I need a lot of drinks. I can't do this anymore. I'm tired, my heart hurts all the time, memories of the awful things I've done continue to flood my mind, I can't stop thinking about drinking, and no matter what those people in AA say, it's not working for me. Sleep comes, but with it the ever-present nightmares that plague me. I wake up screaming.

It's nearly meeting time. While combing my hair and dabbing on makeup, I wonder why I bother. It's true, I feel better physically, look better, but I live in constant turmoil and fear. If the fears don't come out in my waking hours, they invade my dreams. Recently, many of my dreams involve drinking. They're so real I can almost taste the whiskey in my mouth, and I experience the feelings of guilt and remorse upon awakening. I shake my head. I've got to stop thinking. My mind never seems to stop. I know what peace must feel like: the absence of thinking, questioning absolutely everything. At times, I think it would be easier to start drinking again and get it over with. But not tonight. I'll go to the meeting.

Half an hour later, I take a seat across the table from old Bob, a down-to-earth, redneck-looking guy who keeps his AA program simple. Something comes over me, and I pour my heart out about all my woes, how unfair life is, and how badly I want to drink. Several people share, some sympathetic. Others talk about their own problems, but throughout, I can feel old Bob's eyes on me. When it's his turn, he looks directly at me and says, "One of these days, you are gonna get on your knees, or you're gonna get drunk." Not me!

Day by day I continue the struggle. Angel's doing better. Helen has lost weight, is having trouble swallowing because her body continues to stiffen from the Parkinson's. I am angry, resentful that such a wonderful woman must suffer as she does, little by little losing the ability to enjoy the smallest things in life. I'm pissed that I've come to believe this is it . . . my life, a piece of sober crap. I'm exhausted by the mere thought of what lies ahead.

After a particularly hard day at Helen's house and a hot night of very little rest, I shut down. I've had it. I'm going to get drunk. As soon as I leave work today, I'm going to the bar and getting stinking drunk. It's the only thing that ever worked, and it will still work.

All day, as I bathe Helen, powder her back, brush her hair, do her nails, and help her exercise her neck, the thought of the evening ahead lingers in the back of my mind. Helen asks me if I'm okay. She knows me so well. I assure her I'll be fine. And I will be. For the first time in nearly two and a half years, I will find some relief . . . in a bottle.

My resolve doesn't falter as I drive home, feed the dog, take a shower, and get dressed for my evening out. I open the front door to leave. Suddenly, I hear a voice—not from outside of me, but inside my head. It's as loud as if someone spoke next to me. It says, "The day's gonna come when you are gonna get on your knees, or you are gonna get drunk."

I fall to my knees in the open doorway. Through the sobs emanating from the deepest part of me, I say, "God, help me! Please, help me! I give up." An unfamiliar feeling engulfs me. I feel strong arms wrap around my body, and I know—I know that no matter what happens, it's going to be okay. I am not alone.

13

Signs

UNSHED TEARS POOL IN MY EYES. There is a hush as I look out over a sea of faces. All eyes are on me. I know they are expecting some glorious story about how wonderful it is to be sober. All I have to give them is the truth. Today, it's not wonderful. At this very moment, I want nothing more than to run away, find a dark corner in a bar, and drink. Helen died yesterday. It's the first time I've faced death sober. I've wept until I can't believe I have any tears left, but the pain remains.

A month earlier, I was asked to speak at this annual AA picnic in Flora, Illinois. Honored by the request, I jumped at the opportunity to tell my story. Now, here I stand, paralyzed. People are beginning to whisper in hushed tones. I've got to say something. After drawing in a deep breath and letting it out slowly, I say, "I'm Barb, and I'm an alcoholic. Today, I stand before you a miracle . . . because if I weren't here with you right now, there's a good chance I would be stinking drunk." That got their attention. "I lost someone I dearly loved yesterday. It was the perfect excuse to get drunk. I've used it many times over the years."

For the past three years, attending meetings, spending time with other members, and working the AA program gave me direction and new tools to find a better way of life, but Helen had been my rock in an otherwise shaky, uncertain sober world. I told her things I never told another human being, and she loved me anyway. From her, I learned what it meant to be a lady, to have dignity and self-esteem, to believe there is a purpose. Like Aunt Ruthie, she was sure there was more to me than met the eye. But how will I do it without her?

An hour later, my talk is over. I can barely recall what I said. It's like I was possessed, the words coming through me but not from me. There is applause. People stand, hug me, and shake my hand as I make my way through the crowd. I smile and nod, their words falling on deaf ears. I want to go home. I want to rip off the clothing that feels like it's strangling my body. I want to snuggle up with Angel and sleep away the pain. In the back of my mind, I want to drink. I am exhausted, tired of life kicking me in the ass every time I think things are getting better.

At home, I automatically grab the mail from the mailbox, open the door to let Angel out, and step inside to the absolute quietness of my three rooms. The cardboard boxes stacked in the middle of the living room remind me I'll be moving soon, starting a new life. Panic takes my breath away. I slide down the door to the floor and stare at the boxes. I'm 38 years old, and my entire life is packed in four boxes and a trash bag. What am I doing? What if I do this, start over, allow myself to love fully and completely, and I get stomped on again?

———

I can't move, can't shut the memories out. Eighteen years ago, on March 8, Jon's fifth birthday, we stepped off the bus into a snowstorm in Mattoon, Illinois. We had had to get out of Winslow, Arizona in a hurry. When my abusive husband was hospitalized for a back problem, I put my plan of escape into action. I'd been stealing money from the country club where he worked as a golf pro and I ran the restaurant. I had hocked a ring I found in the kitchen. I had skimmed what cash I could from the purchasing funds for groceries, always careful not to get caught. No sooner had he been admitted to the hospital, and I was digging my cache out of its hiding place inside the back of a zip-off couch cushion and running out the door to buy bus tickets for Jon and me. Mattoon, Illinois, the only place I knew anyone, far enough away that my husband wouldn't find me and kill me, seemed the logical choice.

With two suitcases, a bread bag full of bacon sandwiches, and a jug of tea, we were on the bus and headed out of town. I tried to appear calm for my son's sake, pretending that we were going on a vacation, while my heart beat so fast I felt like I'd run a footrace. I kept looking over my shoulder out the back window to see if we were being followed. I didn't know what I was going to do, but anything would be better than the way I'd been living. I closed my eyes and felt the tension melt away with the humming of the wheels against the highway as they took me away.

Nervous and excited, my lively son gobbled up the bag of sandwiches in a hurry. By the second day, the food was gone, and money had dwindled to a bit of change. I cased the bus, wondering if I could get away with stealing from the other passengers. If I got caught, we'd be put off. I decided to wait until the next bus stop, where I might be able to do some shoplifting. But what would happen to Jon if I got arrested? When the situation looked hopeless, three sailors got on the bus and sat directly in front of us. Jon, a gregarious child who'd never met a stranger, made friends with them quickly.

After chatting with them, they told me if I wanted to get some rest, they'd keep an eye on Jon. I fell into a deep sleep and woke with a start when I realized the bus was stopped. The sailors were gone, and my son was gone. I was ready to scream when suddenly they all stepped onto the bus laughing, one young man carrying Jon. They handed me a cup of coffee and a wrapped hamburger. I never knew if Jon told them that we were out of food, if they figured it out, or were simply nice young men, but they fed us for the remainder of the trip. They got off the bus a stop before ours, and one of them stuck a few dollars in my hand.

I had to find a place to stay, and a job, quickly. My mom's sister took us in temporarily. She and her husband were great drinkers, so I didn't have any problem getting alcohol. The day after my arrival, I trudged through the snow to the downtown area of Mattoon and went from business to business, inquiring about jobs. Near the end of the main street, two bars sat across the street from each other: the Office and the Oasis. In the Office, I approached Jack, a ruddy-faced Irishman with a disarming smile. He needed a part-time bartender and said I could start the next day. He sent me across the street to see if I could get part-time work at the Oasis, too. He said to ask for Tom.

I'd read about it. I'd heard about it. I thought I'd experienced it. But when Tom turned toward me, our gazes locked and a shock passed through me like I'd been struck by lightning. I shook it off and convinced myself that my fear and exhaustion had caught up with me, making me vulnerable. The last thing I needed in my life at that moment was another man. Besides, he wasn't my type. I'd always gone for tall, brutish men. I reminded myself where that had gotten me: homeless, penniless, and scared.

Tom hired me part-time. I walked back to my aunt's house, relieved I'd found work but confused about my strange attraction to a virtual stranger. I couldn't get him out of my mind— those piercing blue eyes set in a round, baby face, soft brown curly hair beginning to thin on top, not much taller than I, with a muscular body . . . what was I thinking?

————

In a few days, I'll be moving in with Tom, and we are to be married. I'm still astounded by all the odd occurrences that have taken place since I almost went out drinking that day, when I fell to my knees and begged for help. At the AA meetings I was told that if it works today, it will work tomorrow. From that day on, I continued to get on my knees each morning, seeking those fleeting moments of peace. I returned to my meetings with a different attitude. I asked questions. I listened. I came to understand that if I wanted it all, I had to do it all. That meant actually working those steps.

I'd taken the third step that day on my knees, and every day since then. It was time to write out all the crap I did, to own up to my part in it. First, as was suggested to me, I drew a graph of my life by years, peaking up for good points, down for low points, and making a straight line for years when not much happened. It looked like a zigzag pattern on a quilt. Next, it was time to fill in the details. Oh, my God . . . who lives that kind of life? I did, and it was time to face it. I wrote. I wept. I hated myself. I threw up. I wrote some more. In the wee hours of the morning, I put the pencil down. Exhausted, I crawled into bed. Nightmares filled the night.

The following morning, on my knees, I asked this God of which I still had no understanding to give me the strength to complete the task. The papers spread across the metal kitchen table, I paced back and forth, smoking, reliving my tortured life. My part in things? I'd always blamed everyone else for my problems. I didn't think I was lovable because I didn't believe my parents loved me. Of course, I didn't take into consideration how hard I made it for them to love me. I was a stubborn, willful child who would do anything for attention, and that usually involved inappropriate behavior. Although I squeaked by in school with barely passing grades, never doing homework, I was always in trouble. I could blame my brother for that. He was smart, clean, and well-behaved, and all the teachers loved him. When I came along a year later, they were in for a big disappointment. If I couldn't get attention for being good, I figured out how to do it for being bad. Who could live up to my perfect brother anyway?

Never having learned to be a real friend to anyone, I thrived on gossip and secretly enjoyed it when others suffered. After all, why should their lives be any better than mine? As my body began to mature, I realized boys liked me, paid attention to me, wanted to be with me. It was the beginning of a downhill slide that would last for many years. Females became one of two things to me: a threat or a nuisance, depending on what they looked like. I became a friend to none and a sex partner to many. For that one moment during sex, I felt loved—even if it wasn't real.

When sex wasn't enough, when the feeling didn't last, I started getting married in the mistaken belief it might be different. When getting married didn't fulfill my needs, it was time for babies. Except for Jon, my oldest son, the babies failed to thrive. But I kept trying until I reached age 25 and the doctors told me I had completely ruined my insides. They had to remove all my female organs.

I returned to marriage, but wasn't very good at it. I told myself I was a good parent, always made sure Jon was taken care of, that the reason I failed at marriage was because I picked the wrong men, men who couldn't give me what I wanted—but the truth was that in every relationship I'd had, my needs superseded those of whoever else was involved, including my kid.

I never considered my child when I went off with married men, when I got drunk and didn't show up for school functions, or showed up with booze on my breath at a parent-teacher conference. I didn't think about how I was teaching Jon to cope with life's problems by running away, drinking, using drugs, lying, and conning people. I blamed my husbands when I cheated with other men, drank myself into oblivion, and wrecked cars time and again. I blamed God for every death in my life. I carried a me-against-the-world attitude, and I inevitably came up on the short end of the stick. I deserved to act out, or at least I thought so until I faced my fourth step.

Jack had told me to watch for patterns as I wrote. The patterns became obvious, but hard to accept. I didn't have a clue how to act like a decent human being, wife, or parent. I didn't know how to relate to men—any man—without sex being involved. I had a part in absolutely everything that happened to me. I'd had choices, but chose to take what I believed was the easier way out. Those decisions may have been easier at the time, but they were sure making it harder now. Yet I felt like I was over my greatest hurdle. I'd written it all out, holding nothing back . . . even those secrets I was going to take to my grave.

The following day, sheets of paper in hand, I went to Jack's house to complete my fifth step. I did it. I admitted to God and another human being the exact nature of my wrongs. At home, I began making out the list of persons I'd harmed. Although I was willing to make amends to them, many were dead, and others had been out of my life for years and I had no way of knowing how to contact them. The following weeks were spent visiting cemeteries, writing letters and burning them, praying for the ability to make amends, and actually making the amends I could. Each day, I returned to my knees and turned everything over to a God of my understanding. The last thing I turned over was Tom and my feelings for him. Shortly thereafter, he stopped calling. I knew it was finally over and I could get on with my life.

———

About seven months later, the phone rang. It was Tom. He said he hadn't had a drink in six months and would I have a cup of coffee with him. Stunned, I agreed, but as soon as I hung up the telephone I felt the fear creep in. What did he want? What would he say? How would I feel? Was this another ploy on his part to get me back and then start drinking again? How would I know what to do? I sunk to my knees and said, "God, I need your help. Please, give me a sign."

———

My heart pounding, nausea threatening, like a teenager on her first date, I pulled clothes off hangers, trying on one thing after another. I wanted to look good, but not too obvious. I finally settled on a blue chambray shirt and jeans. Hands shaking, I arranged my hair and applied a little makeup. I'd noticed I didn't have to wear nearly as much since I quit drinking. Ready, I stood at the window, watching for Tom's El Camino, smoking one cigarette after another. When he pulled up, I said, "Oh, God, please keep me from doing something stupid."

I fought the urge to run outside and jump in the car. I waited until he got out and knocked on my door and hoped I seemed calm and unaffected when I opened it. "Are you ready?" he said. "Let me grab my purse," I responded. I didn't carry a purse for years while I was drinking because I often got so drunk I lost it. I grabbed up the denim bag and followed him to the car. We made small talk on the few miles to Mt. Zion, a small town nearby. I talked about Helen, my work, and Angel. He talked about mutual friends from years ago that I hadn't stayed in touch with.

The restaurant was one of those self-serve places where customers go to the counter, order, pay for their food and drink, and then, when a number is called out, pick up the food. We ordered. Tom pulled out his billfold to pay. It caught my eye. It was the leather billfold Jon made for him when he was in Cub Scouts many years ago. He opened it, and I saw a picture of Jon inside. At that moment I knew the truth. I'd been given my sign.

14

The Retreat

I'M ALONE IN TOM'S HOUSE. Fear grips me. What am I doing? What makes me think I can do this? I don't know what I'm supposed to do with myself. It's the first time in my life, since I was a kid, that I don't have to work. It only took a half hour to clean the house after Tom left this morning. It's only a few years old—Tom and some friends got drunk and burned the original house down over the Fourth of July four years earlier. I light a cigarette, step out on the upstairs deck off the master bedroom, and gaze at the picturesque lake. It's beautiful here—so what is wrong with me?

It's hard to fathom that soon I will be living in this house as Tom's wife, that I no longer have to worry about scraping together enough money to pay the rent, keep my old car running, figure out how to eat and feed the dog, or find out where my next smoke will come from. The only time I've ever been in houses this nice was to clean them. All my life, I wondered how others got to live in nice places, what they did if they didn't have to struggle for every penny, why life was so unfair—and here I am.

From the back of the house, I can see the A-frame across the cove where Tom, Jon, and I lived together for two years after I got out of the nuthouse. It was about half the size of this house and not nearly so grand, but a safe haven for Jon and I while we were trying to escape an ex-husband who was stalking me. Jon loved it there. He had his own bedroom upstairs, a lake for swimming just outside the door, decent clothes to wear to school, and he absolutely adored Tom.

I, on the other hand, had a big problem. I was in therapy, going to college, and trying to stay sober. Tom continued to drink. It was a disaster. Because I hadn't had any schooling since the eighth grade and I'd had so much shock therapy that my memory was shot, school was a daily struggle. At times I couldn't remember how to spell the simplest words or connect meanings with words. I carried a dictionary with me to classes every day.

While Tom was out running the bars, coming home drunk and sick from days of drinking and not eating, I was trying to work through my demons with a psychologist. I always thought it odd that I couldn't actually remember growing up . . . birthdays, special holidays, people, or exact circumstances. I could recall being very small, but after that there was a huge gap. It was like one day I was 5 years old and the next 15, with only sporadic memories in between. The therapist suggested hypnosis.

———

I shake my head. This is not a time I want to revisit. I have got to stop thinking about the past, what was done to me. I resolved what I could when I did my fourth and fifth steps, and past events can no longer hurt me or affect my life if I don't let them. It's time to live in the moment and move forward. Soon I'll be attending a spiritual retreat with my lady sponsor, Skippe, and a couple of other AA members. That should be fun. I don't think Tom understands my need to go, but he seems to accept that it's what I want to do. I told him when I agreed to marry him that my AA has to come first—because unless I'm sober, nothing else works in my life. We'll be married in less than a month, so I have time to make sure he meant what he said when he told me it wouldn't be an issue.

Early Friday morning, I jump in Skippe's car, excited about the new experience ahead. I've never been to a retreat, but I've attended many AA functions and always enjoy them. Something happens when I'm around other AA members. I can let my guard down, enjoy a comfort I've never known before, not even in the bar. There is an instant bond among these people, because we are all struggling together for the same thing—to live our lives sober.

My excitement wanes as Skippe and I pull into the parking lot in front of a rather austere brick building in Quincy, Illinois. I try to shake off an odd feeling of doom that settles in my heart, but it is only reinforced when we are shown to our cells. In the small windowless room with two cots and two small dressers, I realize this is not what I imagined it was going to be. I want to go home. If I had my own car, I would leave right now.

The shrill ring of a bell startles me. I run out into the hallway and right into Skippe. She says, "It's time for the orientation meeting." I follow her, and others, into a large room fitted out with rows of metal folding chairs. As the group of about fifty settles into chairs, mine in the farthest corner of the back of the room, a priest steps up to a podium. I know he's supposed to be in recovery from addiction, but he's still a priest. I've never met a priest. I wonder: if this spiritual stuff really works, and he's supposed to be some minion of God, how in the world did he become addicted to booze? Maybe he drank too much of the sacramental wine, I think, and chuckle at my cleverness.

I've been around AA long enough to know it's not religious, but somehow in this building, half-listening to this priest drone on about what to expect over the next few days, the mood feels religious. I don't need this crap. My life is good. I'm doing fine. I bet the priest can't imagine all that I've overcome. I don't believe there's anything he can tell me that I don't already know. Shit, I could probably tell him a few things. This whole thing is stupid. Two and half days left—a piece of cake. I'll never do this again.

Why is everyone staring at me? The woman next to me whispers, "We are counting off. You're number 5." I say my number, and the count continues until everyone has a number. A bell rings. I follow the other number fives into a smaller room near the front of the building. I might have to be there, but I don't have to participate. They can't make me talk. I bet I could share some of my story and really blow their little minds.

A tall, thin woman with a bush of red curly hair says, "I'd like to discuss character defects." I slump in my chair, arms crossed over my chest. That's one thing I don't have to talk about. I didn't have to work the defects steps because once I got sober, I quit doing those things. I don't cheat, lie, steal, or abuse others anymore. I never did understand the purpose of steps 6 and 7. How could addicts continue to behave the same way after the addiction is removed? I'll listen, but I'm not going to participate.

Halfway through the meeting, a heavyset man with dark-rimmed glasses, wearing black slacks and a yellow shirt, enters through the front door and takes an empty seat across from me. He stares at me. I shift in my chair, find myself gripping the edges of the metal seat with my hands. Who is this guy? Why is he here? Is he here to see me? When the bell rings, indicating it's time to return to the main room, I stay in my chair. So does he. We gaze at each other for a moment before he gets up and moves to the chair next to me. Confused, I smile nervously.

He wraps my small hand in his large, beefy one, and says, "I'm Brother John."

"Barb," I stutter.

"What are you doing here?" he says.

"I . . . uh . . . came with my sponsor."

He smiles, still holding my hand. I pull it away, instantly feeling bereft at the loss of contact with the warm secure hold he had on me. What am I doing? Why don't I get up and leave? "What are you doing here?" he repeats.

I can't hold back the tears streaming down my face. "I don't know."

"What happened to you, my dear?"

Between sobs, I blurt out my story, ending with, ". . . and my kids are all dead, I've been divorced five times, and I'm supposed to get married again, and I don't know what I'm doing, or if I can do it."

Brother John puts his arm around me and pulls me to him. I weep into his shirt like someone close to me has just died. He says, "I think you need to spend some time with Father Ted. You need to talk to him one on one."

I don't like Father Ted. I don't want to spend time with him. I want to stay here, enveloped in Brother John's embrace, safe and secure. But I nod. "I'll talk to him about you," Brother John says. "Now go and get some rest."

In my cell, I can't get the strange encounter from my mind. I'm not sure what happened. More tears come. I don't know why. I sleep undisturbed until the supper bell rings. At one of the long tables, I pick at my food, unable to taste it, to enjoy the homemade soup and hot bread, shutting out the noises of others around the table. I want to go back to bed, to pull the covers up to my neck, and to sleep until it's time to go home. I want to go home. I don't belong here.

The following morning, I see that a note has been slipped under the door. I have an appointment with Father Ted after the morning get-together. All through breakfast and the morning meeting, I debate about going. For some reason, I trust Brother John, a virtual stranger whom I know nothing about. I'll go. If I don't like it, I can leave. I'm not a prisoner here. In fact, I don't know why I'm still here—except that I have no way to leave.

After a couple of deep breaths, I knock on Father Ted's office door. He bids me enter and motions to a chair across from him. "John said he thought you needed someone to talk to," he says. "Do you?"

"Actually, I'm feeling a lot better today. Sometimes things get overwhelming, and I'm not sure what to do."

"What kind of things are overwhelming you?"

When he hears my story, he'll be amazed that I lived through it, that I am sober and moving on with my life. I pour out my childhood trauma, the tragedies that plagued my life for so many years, how I reacted to all those things, and how well I'm doing since I got in AA. "I think I've resolved everything pretty good, except for the deaths of my children, and I'm a bit anxious about getting married. You know, divorce never seemed like a bad thing before I sobered up, but now . . ."

He's thoughtful before he says, "Let's talk about your children."

"I had a baby when I was 15. He was healthy. Then, I had a baby girl when I was 17. She was premature, and so little. I thought she wouldn't die, but she did. I watched her struggle for every breath she took. I prayed every day all day, but she died. I had a baby boy when I was 19. The same thing happened. Right after that my mom, who was an alcoholic and hooked on prescription drugs, committed suicide. I lost a child when I was in my twenties, and then they did an emergency hysterectomy so there would be no more children. But I had my first son, Jon. When he was 15, he was killed. It was hard enough when the other kids died—at least I had him. I carry the pain of his death with me every day. Sometimes it washes over me like a giant wave, nearly consuming me. I don't think I will ever be able to let go of the pain or the guilt."

Father Ted sits quietly as I ramble on about what a bad mother and wife I've been; how I didn't take care of myself when pregnant; how I raised Jon to be like me, a runner, an addict; how I taught him it was he and I against an unfair world. When I pause to take a breath, Ted says, "Hell no, Barb, you can't let go of that pain. If you do, you'll never have a reason left to drink, to self-destruct again."

What? Who the hell does he think he is? No one speaks to me this way. I don't think this guy is a real priest. Can priests say "hell"? I stand, glare at him, and slam out the door. I don't have to put up with this shit.

In my cell, I pace back and forth. I hate this room. I hate rooms without windows. They remind me of the basement of our old house. Things happened to me there. Bad things. I've got to get out of here. Outside, I take in great gulps of fresh air and begin walking, with no idea of where I'm headed. As my mind questions everything, I walk faster until I find myself outside a bar. I can hear music, the people laughing and talking, and remember what it was like to find oblivion in those places. The priest's words come back to haunt me. I'm going back there. I'm going to confront him.

This time, I walk through the door without knocking. "How could you say that to me?" I blurt out, and before he can answer, I say, "You have no idea what my life's been like, what I've lived through. I needed your help, and you judged me."

He sits in silence until I finish my tirade, then says, "Barbara, anything that causes you that much pain, that you hang on to that hard, you're getting something out of it. If you ever want to find real peace, you have to figure out what it is."

The words sink in, calming my rage. I drop into a chair. "What do you mean?" I mutter. "I don't want to hurt anymore, but how do I stop it?"

Two hours later, I leave the office, return to my cell, lie down on the cot, and consider what the priest shared with me. Is he right? Could it all be that simple? He said that God wants me to be happy and to have everything I want in life as long as I don't forget where I got it. He said that when I go to God and sincerely ask for forgiveness, but then refuse to forgive myself, I have set myself above God—that when God forgives me, it's like he buries it and it's forgotten, but I keep digging it up and messing in it. He said that if I ever let go of the pain of my mistakes and my losses, I will never have an excuse left to drink, drug, or anything else self-destructive. Apparently, according to him, my defects of character are anything that keeps me from the peace, serenity, and happiness that this God wants for me.

I spoke with Father Ted about my fears about getting married for the sixth time. He informed me that it was time to let go of the past—because I couldn't go back and change it, but I could learn from it. This time, he told me, when you stand in front of the minister with your husband-to-be and you say those vows, you need to hear what you're saying and mean it. He said until I could do that, and not see marriage as a temporary situation, I should remain single.

I told him I wasn't sure I knew how to be a good wife. He laughed and said there was no manual for that, but the best advice he could give me was to mind my own business, to leave God and others, including my husband, to theirs. He said that no matter what I think, what I say, what I do, or how much I worry, other people make their own choices, and they aren't always about me. If I want to be free to choose, I must give that right to others without harsh judgment and criticism. If I truly believed in a God, it's time to understand that as much as I think I am where I am for a reason, others are where they are for a reason, too, and I'm not on a need-to-know basis.

In the backseat of the car on the way home, I close my eyes and think of all I was told. For the first time in years, I feel like I've finally buried my children and let go of my anger toward my mother for leaving me the way she did. I know it's time to take a hard look at the sixth and seventh steps and the character defects that continue to hold me back.

A line in the big book enters my mind. It tells me that in order to know peace, I must stop fighting everything and everyone. I know that includes myself. What a concept.

15

The Dream

WHEN I THINK LIFE CAN'T GET ANY BETTER, IT DOES. The past two years—being married to Tom, the love of my life, living in a beautiful home on a lake, not having to work for a living, or worry about paying bills—have been glorious. I'm having a real life, and I stand in awe of it on a daily basis.

It's time for me to do more. I've had my education all these years and have never done anything with it. Today, Tom is taking me for a job interview with a judge to become a parole officer. Excited, I dress in my best black pantsuit with a white blouse, take time with my makeup, don understated jewelry, and we're on our way. I can picture myself doing this job, helping people who are trying to make their way in the world after paying their debt to society. They aren't that much different from me. The big difference is that they got caught.

Two hours later, we're on our way home. I know I got the job if I want it. Tom says, "You don't seem very excited." I'm not. Although the interview went well, I had no idea what went into being a parole officer: being on call all the time, having to carry a weapon, juggling huge caseloads. After explaining these things to Tom, he says, "What would you do if you could do anything you want?"

For years I've had a secret dream. I've never said it out loud, but I trust Tom not to laugh at me. "I always wanted to be a costume designer," I say and wait breathlessly for his response. He asks if I think I could make any money at it. I don't know. Over the years I made extra money turning old clothes into costumes, but to make a business out of it . . . I just don't know. I shrug my shoulders.

My mind works furiously, and questions tumble through my head. I slip out of bed, through the sliding doors, and out onto the deck. As I stare at the golden reflection of the moon against the water, I consider the discussion Tom and I had over coffee when we arrived home. "God, can I really do this?" I whisper.

Tom's strong arms wrap around my waist. He says, "Want to go for a swim?" I nod. One of our favorite things to do in the heat of the night, when the rest of the world is sleeping, is go skinny-dipping in the lake. I love the feeling of being naked in the water, of holding each other under the stars, laughing and playing like children. As the lake water sloshes around us, I wrap my legs around Tom's waist. He holds me close and says, "You can do this. If it doesn't work, you can do something else. You'll never know if you don't try." My heart swells. I've never been with a man who believed in me the way Tom does—who wanted to help me realize my dream. It has been quite a day: starting out to be a parole officer and ending up imagining myself as a costume designer.

By early October 1987, Broadway Bazaar Costumes is open for business. The past few months have been an excited whirlwind of activity. After ruling out several available buildings for one reason or another, we decided to utilize the old apartments on the second floor of Tom's two bars. While Tom and some of his friends carried out the big items—like refrigerators, old beds, and falling-apart furniture—from the four apartments that had been used for everything from a flophouse to storage, I scoured the thrift shops and garage sales for usable items to convert into costumes.

Our days were spent cleaning and painting the biggest room at the top of the steep staircase, installing a dressing area and office, and getting the bathroom in order. All other rooms were left behind closed doors, available when I needed more space. Late into the night, armed with a variety of dyes, threads, and needles, I created the costumes and accessories to be rented out.

Tom and I moved our bed into the guest bedroom. The master bedroom was converted into a workspace, where thirty papier-mâché heads sat here and there, drying out. One day, as I worked with heavy tinfoil making ears, noses, chins, and eyelids to be attached to the heads before I covered them with fabric, our neighbors and dearest friends, Tom and Jacqui, stopped by with a surprise. They had bought me a treadle sewing machine at an auction. I'd never used a sewing machine before. The simplicity of the old machine called to me. Besides, my fingertips were sore from pushing needles through fabric. I could barely wait until they were out the door to start playing with it.

———

Tom and I stand in the middle of the room, admiring all that we've accomplished. Over a hundred costumes grace the walls leading up to the twenty-foot metal-tiled ceiling. My beloved sewing machine, which has saved me so much time and effort, sits off to one side. When I'm not busy, I can continue working on more costumes. Now, all I need is customers.

Every time the buzzer goes off, indicating someone coming through the downstairs door, my heart speeds up and anxiety overtakes me. I wonder what people will think of what I've done. Will they pay money to rent my creations? Are they good enough? The buzzer sounds. I stare at the open doorway. It's Tom again. I sink back into my chair.

A week before Halloween, I say to Tom, "I think I may have made a mistake." Except for a few people who've wandered up the staircase out of curiosity, I haven't had one customer. He takes me by the shoulders, and says, "Are you having fun?" It has been great. I could spend all day every day making costumes and love every minute of it. "Yes," I respond. He hugs me and says, "Then that's all that matters. The rest will just be gravy."

Four days before Halloween, the gravy begins to pour in. I can barely keep up with the customers, all clamoring for a custom costume to wear to work, to a party, to a haunted house. My head reels from all the compliments, my purse bulges with cash, and I'm having the time of my life. It's a bittersweet happiness, as I wish Jon was here—how he would have loved this! The last costume I made him was of a member of the band KISS. He was 13 years old. He was the hit of the party in the open-front black jumpsuit, his face painted black and white, wearing a black punk wig. Every time he stuck his tongue out as far as he could, we would scream with laughter.

I have a plan. When we lock the doors Halloween night, we're going to buy leftovers at enormously discounted prices at the chain stores. I need more material, and especially accessories that I can't make myself. Excitement vibrates through my body as we amass our treasures. With the latex heads, wigs, feather boas, makeup, and other odds and ends, I will be able to give my customers a better selection. I can hardly wait to get started on the costumes I'm already making in my mind.

———

After three years in business, I can't make costumes fast enough to fill all the orders for custom work. Everyone wants something special. I don't have time to breathe, let alone pray or attend meetings. I'll get back to it when things slow down. Today I have to hurry because I have a lot to do before Jacqui and I leave on a trip to Chicago to attend the Halloween and party trade show. I start down the staircase in my fabulous home, and half-way down, I think, damn, I'd like to have a drink. The thought stops me in my tracks. My mind's eye searches the house for alcohol. I know I made Tom get rid of all of it, but maybe he missed something. No, there's nothing . . . except the cough syrup up in the bathroom. My God, what am I thinking?

Words I've heard my friend George say so many times at the meetings spring into my mind. "I'm an alcoholic. I'll be an alcoholic until the day I die, and if I don't keep something between me and the bottle, I will drink again." What had I been keeping between me and the bottle? Tom? Work? My good life? Apparently, at that moment at least, it wasn't working. I drag myself down the stairs, pick up the telephone receiver, and punch in my sponsor's number. God, I hate to admit that after six years of sobriety, I'm thinking about drinking. Maybe she won't answer. She does.

As soon as I hear her voice, I start to sob. She says, "It's the most normal thing in the world for an alcoholic to want to drink. You never needed an excuse before, and you don't need one now. Have you been doing meetings?" I admit I hadn't done any recently, but I am busy trying to get my business going, taking care of the house, Tom, and the dog. "Well," she says, "If you start drinking again, you won't have to worry about any of those things, will you?"

I tell her about my upcoming trip, that I have to leave early in the morning. She says, "Good. That means you have time to go to a noon meeting and an evening meeting today." I barely get the word "but" out when she continues, "What could be more important than your sobriety?" I was going to do some shopping, get some new clothes for the trip. I guess I can wear what I've got.

Two hours later, I'm sitting around a long table in the Al-Anon Club where they have several meetings a day. When the chairperson asks if anyone has a topic, I say, "I'm Barb, and I'm an alcoholic. I am living the best life I've ever had. There is absolutely nothing wrong, and I thought about drinking today."

16

Graves'

. ————————————

"SOMETHING'S WRONG WITH ME," I tell my doctor. "I'm hot all the time. My skin feels like it's on fire. I wake up every day with my eyes feeling like they have sand in them."

He consults his chart and tells me that my blood tests look okay, my estrogen level is good, but that some women simply have a harder time with menopause than others. I know this isn't menopause. I've begun to wonder if I'm going to be one of those people who bursts into flames while lying in bed. I saw a story about it on television. Frustrated by another disappointing appointment with the doctor and clutching the eye drop samples in my hand, I return to the shop.

Halfway up the staircase, my heart is pounding out of my chest. I can't do this—not today. As I turn the CLOSED sign outward in the window at the front door and drive slowly home, I wonder, why? Why is this happening to me now? I've worked so hard over the past eight years, cleaning and painting each room, filling them with costumes. I've won the respect of the costuming community by competing at the National Costumer's Association conferences and winning many awards. Big corporations and ad agencies from as far away as Manhattan have called, requesting specialty costumes. I've shipped costumes all the way to London, had some on the stage in Las Vegas. My business is thriving. But I think I may be dying.

As soon as I get in the door of the house, I strip off my clothes. Every seam burns my skin. I know the neighbors will think I'm nuts because it's not even Easter yet, but I slip on a bathing suit, go out to the lake, and walk into the frigid water up to my neck. It's heaven. Numbness begins to set in. I return to the house and wrap a sheet around my body. I can't stand the touch of a towel. It feels like sandpaper. Needing to lie down, I stare at the staircase that leads to the bedroom. I know if I go up, my heart will race. Instead, I spread a sheet on the couch, lie down, but sleep won't come. There is something terribly wrong with me, and no one seems to know what. Tears spring to my eyes, soothing them better than any drops can.

A car door slams. Tom comes in the back door. He knows there is something wrong because today I should have been setting up displays of rabbits and religious costumes for the churches and working on the Roman soldiers that need to be completed. I need to pull myself together. I have a lot to get finished. The phone has been ringing off the wall. "What happened?" he says and sits next to me. I fill him in on what the doctor said. He has no idea what to do, either.

"I have to find something to wear to work," I say. "Something that doesn't irritate my skin, and isn't hot." At home, I live in a sheet and can barely stand it. At work, I keep the air-conditioning on so high in the main room that I nearly freeze the customers. It's the only way I can function at all. I assure Tom I'll figure it out. I'll make some adjustments, and everything will be fine.

By Halloween I can't leave the main room, but I've hired two young women to help out, and my friend Jacqui is working with me. I must be quite a sight, dressed in a long, flowing Hawaiian-style dress, hair straggling, dark glasses. The dress keeps the rashes on the inside of my thighs from bleeding. My hair, which I have little of since the shock therapy, is falling out daily. My eyes hurt all the time, and light makes them worse. I've been back and forth to the doctor many times, but I'm not getting any better.

Halloween, my favorite holiday and the time I make more than half of my yearly income, is grueling. I can't wait for it to be over. Since the business has grown, I have very few breaks from one holiday to the next. People are already reserving costumes for Thanksgiving and Christmas, and I've turned down a lot of custom work because I can't do it.

As is our routine, Tom and I hit the stores that carry seasonal Halloween items, buy them out at huge discounts, and use them as fresh product for the following year. I know I shouldn't go with him this year, but it's not like the stuff will be there later. Against his wishes, I insist on going. At a mall in Champaign, Illinois, we walk through the door, take a few steps, and my heart begins to pound. I have to sit down. Tom says, "That's it. You're going to the hospital."

At Carle Hospital, the young intern asks me if I've ever been tested for a thyroid condition. I don't know. I've had a lot of blood tests, I tell him, but I don't know anything about my thyroid. He runs the test. We wait. Another doctor enters my cubical, an older man followed by an intern. The doctor says, "Mrs. Rogers, you have Graves' disease."

What is that? Am I going to die? Am I going to have to live the way I've been living for the rest of my life? "There are two courses of treatment I can recommend," he continues. "We can remove your thyroid, or you can have radioactive iodine, which will shut your thyroid down."

"Don't I need my thyroid?" I say. The doctor assures me there is medication that will help. "When do I have to decide?" I ask. He and the intern exchange a knowing look before he tells me that he suggests I get it taken care of right away. I don't know what to do. "If you decide on the radioactive iodine, I can make a call and get you into a hospital that does that procedure . . . today."

I sit in stunned silence on the four-hour drive to Barnes Hospital in St. Louis. Tom touches my hand. I don't know how just the touch of his hand makes me think things will be okay, but it does. I'm scared. He knows I'm scared. But he also knows it has to be done. I can't go on the way I am much longer. The doctor said that without treatment I will begin to lose it mentally and eventually go into cardiac arrest. My mind screams: Why? Why now? Why, when I finally have a life, am happier than I've ever been before? What did I do to deserve this? I've been good, worked hard, and now this. I don't get it.

As if he can read my mind, Tom says, "We're gonna get through this. At least we know what it is, and they can do something about it." I'm having a hard time feeling grateful, but I force a smile and nod. What are they going to do to me at Barnes? Is radiation like chemo? Will it make me sick? I remember how Aunt Ruthie was vomiting so much she had to spend the night next to the toilet after she had chemo. I used to buy her marijuana to smoke before and after a treatment to help with the nausea. Will I have to smoke pot? I can't. I'm in recovery from addiction. What will I do?

There is no waiting around at Barnes. Tom handles the paperwork as I'm hustled into a room for a quick examination and explanation of the procedure. It sounds simple enough . . . no needles, no machines. I'm moved to a sparsely furnished white room. A female technician dressed in protective clothing enters with something small in her hands. Carefully, she sets it down on the table in front of me. It's a lead box surrounding a white paper cup with clear liquid and a straw. "You need to drink all of this, but be careful not to spill even a drop. If you do, it will contaminate the room." How strange that I can put something in my body that can't be loosed in the room. It's either this or they'll cut my throat and take my thyroid out. I drink.

The technician says, "You think you've been sick, but for a while you are going to get a lot worse. As your thyroid shuts down, you'll have very little energy, you may gain weight, and look out for more hair loss." I may as well shave my head if I lose much more. "We have to make sure the procedure works before you can be put on medication," the technician tells me. I ask about my eyes. She informs me that my eyelids have retracted so much that they no longer close all the way, and that's why they are dry all the time. It seems that often the eyes will get better on their own, so I should wait awhile before seeing an eye surgeon. Eye surgeon? Who said anything about eye surgery?

When I think we're finished, the technician hands me a card and says, "You have to carry this with you at all times. Try to stay out of places like airports because you could set off radar." What?

"You will need to stay as far away from your husband as possible. Don't fix his meals or do his laundry. Do you have your own bathroom?" I nod. "Do you have any pets?" I nod. "Stay away from your pet, and avoid being around children, especially babies." My God, what did they do to me?

On the opposite side of the car, in the backseat as far away from Tom as I can get, I consider all I've been told. I can't believe I can't touch him. And what about poor little Georgie? She'll be devastated. When Angel got so sick that we knew we were going to have to have her put down, our vet called one day and asked me to come to the office. He brought out a badly abused dog that looked like our Angel. She had been beaten, starved, and thrown from a car and was obviously scared to death of people. My heart went out to her. We took her home, and after a lot of medical attention, love, and patience, she came to love and trust us. She won't understand why I can't hold her, why she can no longer sleep next to me. Overwhelmed by an odd feeling, I realize I'm pissed off. I'm tired of every strange thing happening to me.

———

Life becomes a daily struggle. I have barely enough energy to drag myself off the couch. I can't go to meetings, have friends over, or get near my husband because I've got so much radioactive stuff in me that I could shut down someone else's thyroid. I'm tired, I'm lonely, and the anger that germinated that day in the back of the car has begun to fester. I look like crap. One afternoon, as I look at my face in the bathroom mirror, I pick up a razor and shave what little hair I have left on the sides off. A mohawk looks better than the sporadic clumps of thin hair.

I hate doctors. None of the three doctors I see in Champaign have had a Graves' patient. I'm so sick of them saying, "Let's try this." Nothing is working. Horrendous headaches plague me and last for weeks at a time. It feels as if my face is swollen— it even hurts when the wind blows against it. All of a sudden, I start having bad reactions to every medication they give me. The most recent is a pill for cholesterol. I awaken one morning and can barely see. I panic. Tom calls the eye surgeon, who tells us that the pills have caused progressive cataracts. She says they will remove the cataracts, cut my eyeballs open, and put in intraocular implants, one eye at a time. I can't believe a doctor is going to put stitches in my eyeballs. Two surgeries later, I can see, but the pain in my head continues.

I reach a point at which I would do anything to feel better. If I thought dunking my head in a bucket of gasoline would help, I'd consider it. Sitting on the couch next to Tom, I say, "I can't live this way. If they can't do something to help me, I don't know what I'll do." He asks if there is anything he can do. "Get me some pot." Without question, he nods, gets up, and leaves. I know he'll do whatever I ask. Two hours later, he returns with the marijuana. I'm on the phone with my brother in Phoenix. He worked as a registered nurse for many years. I'm telling him about the headaches, my inability to take medication. He says, "You know, this may sound strange, but you might try castor oil."

Castor oil . . . he must be nuts. I hate castor oil. Mom used to give it to us in our juice when we were little. I fed mine to the dog, who constantly had the shits. "Make a hot pack with castor oil, hold it against your face, and massage it in at night," he continues. "It's a natural anti-inflammatory."

Within hours after I apply a steaming wet washcloth with castor oil, the pain is tolerable. It's three days later and the swelling is gone. I've seen so many specialists who wanted to cut my face open or medicate me—I can't believe the answer is in a cheap bottle of castor oil. I dial Bill to thank him for the information and ask how he knew the castor oil would work.

Bill says, "I was at a party the other night. Some people were talking about Edgar Cayce's books, and I remembered that he talked about castor oil being an anti-inflammatory. I figured it was worth a try."

Goose bumps travel up my arms. It's a God thing, my mind screams at me, but I push the thought away. Bill was just in the right place at the right time. My friend Neva used to say there is no such thing as coincidence, that everything happens for a reason. I can't imagine any good reason for this illness.

17

Healing

SOME DAYS DEATH SEEMS JUST A HEARTBEAT AWAY and possibly preferable to the way I live. The doctors assure me that I will get better, but it may take up to four years. I'm not sure I can last. I didn't smoke the pot because the castor oil is helping my head, but it feels as if I have nothing left with which to fight back. I'm ugly, I'm fat, I'm exhausted all the time, and I'm mad at God. How could he give me the best life I'd ever had, then rip it away? I quit praying a long time ago.

It has been a long day. I've pulled out all the stops, allowing myself to relive all the pain and loss of the past, bringing me to a deep depression. I don't want to drink, but am not sure I want to live any longer. I would call one of my AA friends, but I'm sick of their platitudes. If one more person tells me that this too shall pass, that there is a reason for everything, that I need to work my maintenance steps, I think I'll puke. What do they know? They aren't living through this.

My husband, who has a vending business on top of owning several bars, is out on a machine call. I don't know where, or if it's a pinball machine, a pool table, or a poker machine, but it doesn't matter. I'm alone in the house except for Georgie, who loves me no matter how I look or how irritable I can be. As darkness descends, I lie across the bed, but sleep won't come. I try to hang on to my dark thoughts; however, the steps, all the messages I've been given over the years, slip into my mind. I know what I've been told. I know what to do. Why can't I do it?

In an attempt to clear my mind, I step out on the upper deck and stare unseeing at the star-filled night. I wish Tom were here. God, he deserves better than this. He's been great, taking care of me, running me back and forth to doctors—keeping up with his businesses and mine. The shop is only open by appointment now. Tom goes in when there is a call and rents out costumes. How lucky I've been to have had this time with him. As soon as the thought hits, I understand what I need to do.

"Dear God," I wail through my tears, "I am so sorry." I have been given so much, have known real love, found a happiness I never imagined, and if I died today, I will have had more than I ever dreamed of. "Can you ever forgive me for being such an ungrateful ass?" All I've done since I got sick is wallow in self-pity and focus on my limitations. "If you give me another chance, I'll do better. If you want to take me, I'll understand. Thank you for my life." I fall to my knees, just as I had done that day in the doorway of the garage apartment, and say, "Please, God, help me! Help me to understand what you want me to do."

In bed, lying back against the pillow with Georgie at my side, I say, "Now I lay me down to sleep, I pray the Lord my soul to keep. If I die before I wake, it's been quite a ride." I know it's not over. I remember Barbara, a woman from Florida who came to Illinois to visit her mother. She once said that it took everything in her life—every experience, every person, every moment—to bring her to this moment, to the person she is, doing what she's doing. If that's true for her, perhaps it's true for me, too. I wonder what God will have me doing. I may not have a clue about that, but have no doubt about what I shouldn't be doing—and it's time to get into action.

The following morning, I awaken with the anticipation of a child. I slept so soundly that I didn't hear Tom come home. He comes down the stairs to a breakfast I actually cooked— he won't have to eat at the truck stop this morning. "What's the occasion?" he says and smiles. My heart is nearly bursting with love for him. I want to make amends, to say I'm sorry for the way I've been acting. He's hard to apologize to because he doesn't expect it, but I need to say the words. The first of the maintenance steps tells me to continue to take a personal inventory, and when I'm wrong, to promptly admit it.

There are others I've offended, not appreciated, from whom I've withheld my help and affection—even my compassion. My harsh judgment and lack of understanding for others has grown in direct proportion to the pain and anger that I feel. I'd been sponsoring nine people in early recovery before I got sick. Most of them have stopped calling. I couldn't find the empathy I needed to listen to their problems because I thought mine were worse. The things I've said come back to choke me. I have some work to do.

I kiss Tom before he leaves for the day and immediately get out pen and paper. I begin to write it all out. I've learned not to beat myself up for past wrongs, but to do what I can to make the situations better and move forward. I call my sponsor, to whom I've been cool, off-putting, argumentative, and at times rude. She's understanding, and even attempts to justify my actions. I'm not having it. I know that I've done her wrong. As with Tom, I must say the words.

With each phone call, each face-to-face encounter, I begin to feel better. On my knees each morning, I turn my will and life over to the God of my understanding. I am rewarded with the peace that has eluded me for so long. My medical situation has not yet improved, but my attitude about it has changed.

Exhausted from making the beds and cleaning my bathroom, I lie down on the couch. Tomorrow, I'll dust and clean Tom's bathroom. Tom always said that I do everything like I'm killing snakes. He wasn't wrong. We just didn't understand that there was a medical explanation for it—I'd been running on high octane in the form of too much juice flowing out of my thyroid, giving me a false sense of energy. Now it's time to accept my limitations and focus on what I can do—not what I can't do.

———

Tom said the strangest thing this morning over breakfast—he asked if I still wanted to write a book. I must have mentioned that I did at one time or another. I laughed and said that I would, but I didn't know the first thing about writing. So many people have told me I should write a book about my experiences, and secretly I've always wished I could. But it's so far out of my abilities that I can't imagine it as a real possibility.

Tom comes home with a big box in his arms. It's filled with a used typewriter, ribbons, and paper. "What is this for?" I say, surprised at the gift. "Now, you can write that book," he responds. I didn't mean it. I couldn't do it. "You'll never know if you don't try," he says. "What have you got to lose?" He means well. Maybe . . . what if . . . no, I'm not that smart. At least I can use it to write letters.

We set up the typewriter in the spare bedroom downstairs. Each day I walk past it. I begin to wonder—why not try it? But what would I write? The only books I've read for years are the romance novels Helen got me hooked on.

One afternoon, sitting at the desk chair, I run my fingers over the keys. I haven't typed since I was in junior high school, and that was only for six weeks. Do I remember how? I insert paper and type, "Now is the time for all good men to come to the aid of their country." I like the feel of it, the sound of the keys clicking.

It becomes my habit to awaken early, go downstairs, make coffee, and do my morning prayers and meditation. I feel drawn to the typewriter. Tom won't be up for a couple of hours. Heavily sugared coffee, an ashtray, my cigarettes and lighter on the desk beside the machine, I stare at the clean white sheet of paper. It's kind of like looking at a piece of clothing that I will convert into a costume. If I can create something beautiful from a plain dress, perhaps I can do it on paper, too. An idea takes hold. My fingers move quickly over the keys.

My days pass by faster. I'm feeling better and working steadily. The doctor has finally gotten my medication at the right level. Although I'm not making costumes, I've gone back to work half days and accompany Tom into town when there are appointment calls for costumes. Each day, I set reasonable goals to keep the house clean and organized. But the best part of my day is early in the morning, when it's just me, my typewriter, and the romance novel I've been working on for months. It's taking shape.

The phone rings. It's Tom. He's coming home with something special for me. I can hardly wait. He's not one to buy presents for holidays and special occasions, says he hates feeling pressured into finding gifts, but he might show up on a Tuesday in the middle of May with a wonderful surprise for me. I wonder what it is today. I listen for the car in the drive, watch out the window. Half an hour later, he backs into the driveway. There are boxes in the back of the El Camino. He hefts the largest box through the door. It's a personal computer!

Excitement builds as we set the computer up on the desk in the living room. It has a word processor, which will make rewrites a lot easier. I'll be able to delete, move things around, do research, and won't have to thumb through the big diction-ary and thesaurus for words and meanings. We work late into the evening, reading instructions and experimenting with the machine. By bedtime, my head hurts.

Excruciating pain pounds in my head by morning. It's the entire right side of my head—my right eye, ear, cheekbone, and down through my neck. Unable to take medication (because if there is one strange side effect or allergic reaction, I get it), I spend the day with the drapes pulled closed in our bedroom, hot castor oil poultices pressed against the side of my face and neck. Over two days of bed rest, only getting up to eat and go to the bathroom, the pain begins to subside.

After a busy morning at the shop, I can't wait to get home to play with the computer. I want to get back to writing my book. I like writing, and it's a good book, as good as some of the ones I've read. I know it will get published—if I ever finish it. But by evening, the pain has returned. I spend more days in bed. This time, I call my doctor, who tells me he wants me to see a neurologist. God, I thought those days were over—but I've got to do something. I agree. A couple of hours later, the nurse calls with an appointment.

Weeks of exams, tests, scans, and lengthy discussions with doctors ensue, reminiscent of the early days before I was diag-nosed with Graves' disease. Yet again, my life is on hold. The doctors' best guess is that I have a nerve problem in my face. One way to cure that would be to cut the problem nerves. I imagine myself taking a bite of a sandwich and it falling out the other side of my mouth. I don't think so. There's got to be a better solution. God and I need to have a little chat about this. I'm not angry, not wondering why, but I need help. I pray for help.

The phone rings early in the morning. I drag myself from the comfort of my bed. An unfamiliar voice asks, is this Barb R.? I know it's someone in the program. "Yes," I mumble, thinking it's someone who needs help. The man introduces himself and asks me if I would be willing to speak at an AA anniversary party at a hospital near St. Louis. Some people who have graduated from their treatment program are getting together, and they really want a woman speaker. Without thinking, I agree. My sponsor always told me that when I'm asked to do something like that, God is giving me an opportunity, and I will never know where it might lead me. Since I'm still not driving and Tom is not involved in AA, I call a friend in the program and ask if he will drive me.

Two weeks and several bottles of castor oil later, I'm in the car with four men with whom I've shared years of sobriety, driving through a harsh winter night to the meeting. Physically I'm feeling pretty good, but I'm nervous about speaking. Although I've spoken many times over the years, I still get rattled at the thought of it. I recite some quick prayers on the two-hour ride.

Inside the hospital, we locate the meeting room and step inside. It must be the wrong room. There are long tables draped in white linen and adorned with candles and flowered center-pieces, and people dressed like they are at an awards dinner. A well-dressed man walks up to us and says, "Can I help you?" Apologetically, I tell him we are looking for a group of AA people. "You're in the right place," he says. Oh, my God, this can't be the place. I'm suddenly aware of my attire: blue jeans, a tee shirt, boots, a winter coat, and the ever-present mohawk hairdo. I have no choice. I say, "I'm your speaker."

As we follow the man to a table at the front of the room, I can feel people staring. In all my years, in all the places I've spoken, I've never seen anything like this. Usually it's all very casual—some people even look like they're homeless. Someone should have warned me. Well, I'm here. I've got to speak. I might as well enjoy myself, I think, as I eye the steak dinner set in front of me. Immediately after the meal, the meeting begins with the Serenity Prayer and the reading of steps and traditions. I'm introduced. Hesitantly I take the stage, stand in front of the microphone, and say, "You folks clean up pretty good . . . for a bunch of drunks. I thought I walked into the wrong room." Laughter fills the room. I relax and begin my story: what it was like, what happened, and what my life's like now.

It's important that I share the story of the crisis of faith I endured when I was diagnosed with Graves' disease, what I learned about myself that is helping me deal with what's going on now. At my close, there is a standing ovation. The chairperson encourages others to ask questions or make comments if they wish. One woman stands and says, "You've said so many wonderful things about your husband, we'd like to meet him."

Confused, I look at the table of men who accompanied me. "Oh . . . oh, no, I'm not married to any of them." I don't know if it's what I said or the way I said it, but the crowd roars with laughter.

On the way out, I'm accepting thanks from so many, shaking hands, when a gray-haired gentleman steps in front of me. He hands me a slip of paper and says, "I think you need to see a friend of mine. He's a specialist at Barnes Hospital, and all he deals with is people who've had eye problems like yours. I think he might be able to help you." Before I can respond, one of the men who brought me nearly pushes me out of the room. The weather is getting worse, and it's a long drive home.

I stick the slip of paper in my pocket before taking my seat in the car and don't give it another thought. The guys are laughing so hard about the look on my face when we first walked into the room. The driver says, "When that woman asked about your husband, we should have all stood up and said we were your ex-husbands." They tease me all the way home.

Undressing for bed, I feel the paper in my pocket, pull it out, and tell Tom what the man said. I hate the thought of another doctor, but maybe this one can help me. I don't know. I'm tired, yet I spend a restless night wondering if this is the solution I prayed for.

18

Maui

"FASTEN YOUR SEAT BELTS," THE FLIGHT ATTENDANT SAYS.

"It could be a bumpy ride," I mumble and strap myself in. I have no idea what to expect. The window shade pulled down, I grip the sides of my seat until we're in the air. I remember why I used to drink before I got on airplanes. This thing could fall down and hurt me. At least when I was drunk, I probably wouldn't have noticed.

Irritated at the loud middle-aged couple in the middle and aisle seats next to me—I'm trying to listen to the flight attendant tell us what to do in case of emergency—I grab the laminated card from the seat back abruptly. They keep talking—too subtle. I consider saying something to them, but I have to sit next to them for the next seven hours. No sense pissing them off right away. Damn, I need a cigarette. I rub the nicotine patch. It's not helping much.

As soon as the server cart pulls up, the man and woman order drinks. The woman unscrews the cap from a miniature bottle of gin. I love the smell of gin, could drink glasses of it straight. I watch as she pours it over ice and adds a bit of Squirt. I've got to get out of here. I should have gotten an aisle seat.

In the closet-sized bathroom, I look up at the ceiling and say, "This is a test, right?" I can't drink . . . no, I don't want to drink. I'm about to fulfill a dream, and this time, I'm not going to mess it up. I picture the portable typewriter stowed in the overhead compartment. I'm a published author, and one day, I'll be a well-published novelist. Tepid water cupped in my hands, I splash it onto my face, dry off with a paper towel that has the consistency of a newspaper, and stare into my eyes in the mirror. I can do this. I've worked so hard, overcome so much over the past few years to have this opportunity. I won't give it up for a bottle of booze.

———

After Tom brought home the computer that I thought was the answer to my prayers, the nightmare began. The headache pain, so bad there were not words to describe it, returned with a vengeance. On the second visit to the specialist the gray-haired stranger at the hospital told me about, I am told that some people who have diseases like mine can't look at a computer screen. I'd never considered that that computer could have been causing my headaches.

I tried changing the background color on the computer screen. It didn't work. I wore dark glasses, to no avail. Tom bought a desk with a heavy gray glass top. The computer sat inside, on a sloped shelf. It didn't matter what we did—my head hurt when I used the PC. I knew it was time to give up, to return to the typewriter and complete my book that way. I didn't get angry this time. I decided to look at the whole thing as a challenge instead of a limitation. I could still see, and I could still type.

I finished my 435-page time travel romance novel. It was probably a bit long for a romance novel, but it was so good, I couldn't imagine cutting anything out. At the library and bookstores, I searched for the names of potential publishers, got addresses, made copies, and sent the manuscript out, excited at the prospect of becoming a published author. My mind had already begun to fantasize about what could be. I'd stuck an ad for a writer's conference in Maui on my bulletin board, knowing that someday I'd go there, but not as a wannabe author—as the real thing.

Rejected! Rejected! Rejected! One by one the manuscripts were returned, rejected without telling me why. They were addressed "Dear Author" and ended with "Good luck with your project." I told myself my book was simply too long—they must have liked the story. It had a great plot, based on one of the murder mystery games I carried in my shop. I struggled with a rewrite and sent it out again. Again, I all I got was Rejected! Rejected! Rejected! Disheartened but determined, I rewrote and sent it out again. Rejected! Carefully touching the title page, I placed my manuscript in my desk drawer.

My writers magazine came in the mail. As I thumbed through the pages, an article jumped out at me. It talked about writing about what you know. What did I know? I knew about costuming. What if I did a book about costuming without sewing? I shared my idea with Tom. He always supported whatever I wanted to do and was enthusiastic. We sat down with pen and paper to figure out what I'd have to do. In bed that night, my mind worked so furiously that I barely slept.

My obsessive-compulsive nature kicked in, and in no time I'd set up a room in the house, dragged mannequins home, bought a camera, and packed up secondhand clothes I had stashed in the shop for later use. Pictures of the original garments on the mannequins completed, I began to construct the book. I made the costumes, took the pictures, and kept track of my changes—but there was a problem: how to do the sketches. I had never been able to draw, and to this day I can't make a decent-looking stick figure.

Stumped but not deterred, I ran through several ideas that didn't work until I hit on one that did. At the copy shop, I had the pictures of the original garments blown up to page size, traced over the outline of each garment, and drew in the changes I made to turn it into a costume. All that was left to do was to write. Through the entire process of writing the costume book, I knew that someday I'd return to my novel.

There were only a few publishers of costuming books. I sent the manuscript out. One from Colorado was interested. We spoke on the phone. He informed me that I really needed a theme, not simply a bunch of costumes, but he would be willing to take another look later. I started over, settling on theatrical costumes as my theme.

My dad's sister, Aunt Ellen, died. Dad came to Mattoon, and soon the rest of the family followed. Because of the bad blood between myself and Dad's brother, who'd been my stepdad and the bane of my existence for much of my childhood, I decided not to attend the funeral. Except for Dad, who stayed with Tom and me, everyone bunked with relatives in town. I wanted to go to the funeral for my cousins, but knew that with all of them drinking, there was no way to avoid disaster.

One of my cousins called to tell me that my stepdad wanted to see me. My first impulse was to decline vehemently. My second thought scared the hell out of me. I'd made a pact with God that when any opportunity to make amends presented itself, I would be willing. That moment might be the only opportunity I would have to take care of unfinished business. I agreed to meet with my stepdad at the truck stop in the nearest town. As soon as I hung up the phone, I went to my bedroom, got on my knees, and did some serious praying. I needed help to get through this. An unexpected calmness came over me.

Tom and I arrived first, ordered coffees, and waited. When I saw him and my cousin walk through the door, my stomach lurched for a moment, but I took a deep breath, reminded my-self why I was there, and greeted them as they sat down across from us. I knew my stepdad had been drinking, having seen him in that state—eyes drooping, slightly slurred speech—many times before. He refused to make eye contact with me as he talked. Through his sarcastic remarks and snipes, blaming my mother for his unhappiness, I made amends for all the trouble I'd caused over the years. He agreed that I'd been a pain in the ass, attempted to lay a guilt trip on me about Jon and what a failure I was as a parent and a person, but for the first time, it didn't work. All my life, he'd made me feel bad about myself, told me I'd never amount to anything, that the only thing a man would want me for was my body, and that I was stupid. The last thing I said before we left was, "All I ever wanted was for you to love me . . . and I never thought you did." It was the last amends I had to make. My side of the street was clean.

———

I kept myself busy running the shop, working on the costume book, being active in AA, attending meetings, sponsoring oth-ers, and spending time with Tom and the dogs. I'd never been good at pacing myself and soon began to suffer from exhaustion. Tom suggested we take a trip to Arizona to visit my brother who, with his life partner, had moved to a small mountain community called Yarnell. Even though I'd lived in Arizona for years, I'd never heard of the place before. Reluctant to return to Arizona, where I had done a lot of my drinking, my kids and mother had died, and a couple of my ex-husbands still lived, I said I'd think about it. After speaking to my brother, though, I agreed. He told me that Yarnell, two hours from Phoenix, was a quiet town of 500 residents, mostly retired people, and gay couples. It filled the bill if I wanted to rest and heal.

After I turned my business over to Jacqui and Tom left his with his friend and longtime employee, Gilbert, we packed enough clothes to stay in Yarnell for up to a month. Tom, our two dogs (Georgie, our black-and-white terrier who'd certainly come into her own as a part of our family, and Sammi, a delicate Italian greyhound Tom bought as a companion for me when I was housebound), and I were on our way to Arizona. After three days of driving and two nights in motels, we entered the quaint town set between two mountain ranges: the Weaver Mountains on one side, and the Bradshaws on the other. As per my brother's instructions, we turned right at the post office, took the next left, drove another block, and we'd reached our destination—Bill's house. He'd made arrangements with the lady next door, who would be out of state for some time, to rent us her house for a month.

The month flew by. We went for long walks exploring the area, drove around looking at the unusual houses, and stopped in at the local shops and restaurants. One day while walking uptown, which consisted of a few blocks of businesses along the highway, we stopped at an antique shop set back from the road. When we walked up to it, a large dog emerged from his house, a brightly colored bandana around his neck, and barked. A man stepped out of the trailer behind the shop. I said, "When are you open?" He laughed and said, "When the dog barks." That seemed to be the norm in this odd little community.

I looked back through the window of the car on our way out of town. I'd fallen in love with Yarnell, with its, huge boulders, trees, and the laid-back attitude of its residents. Something about it reminded me of my childhood down on the river. I cried. Tom said, "You know, it would be a good place to spend the winter." Yarnell, originally a gold mining town, was purported to have the most moderate climate in Arizona. "Maybe," Tom continued, "we ought to have Bill keep his eye out for a house. Something not too expensive where we could spend a few months a year."

Within two months of our departure, Bill called to tell us about a house. It was secluded, set in the boulders, and cheap, but it needed some work. I wasn't a stranger to hard work, having worked like a man for most of my life. At a meeting years ago, we were comparing the worst jobs we'd ever had. I won. One particular summer when I was broke, I took a job with a company that cleaned the recreational areas. I rode on the side of a huge trash truck along with some others. We picked up litter around the lakes, camping areas, and fish cleaning stations. The worst part of the job was dealing with the holes in the ground where all the fish guts washed down. They had to be cleaned out with big dip nets. When we opened the heavy wooden door concealing those holes, the smell would have brought a full-grown camel to his knees. All summer, I couldn't get the odor of fish out of my clothes, my skin.

Sight unseen—over the telephone and through the mail—we purchased the house. After the Halloween rush, we returned to Yarnell for the winter. I'll never forget the look on Tom's face when he saw our place for the first time. Crestfallen would be an understatement. He wasn't used to having to fix a place up to live in it—he had no vision—but I did. The house was a mess, but it had great potential. By the end of winter, I'd turned it into a home, but it still required some serious work the two of us were unable to do. We decided to stay longer, to hire workmen to fix the twenty-five leaks in the roof, pour a cement floor in the kitchen, and replace the tile in the kitchen which had been laid on dirt, put a ceiling in a room without one, and spray for critters like scorpions, black widows, and centipedes.

Even before we'd driven back into Illinois, we had decided to move to Yarnell full-time. It took several months of preparation: Tom sold his vending business and leased out his bars, and Jacqui took over my costume shop. We gave away most of our possessions, loaded up my mannequins and costume stuff and the rest of the things we absolutely needed, and were off on a new adventure to a place where hardly anyone knew us, where we had no history with others. We wanted a simpler life, and in Yarnell, we could have it.

Tom helped me finish the costume book. I sent it back to the publisher who'd shown interest in it, got a contract, and was published within the year. I was flying high. Early mornings, before the work started on the house, I got up and typed another rewrite of my romance novel. I hadn't given up on the idea. The organizers of the Maui Writers Conference were having a retreat there for a week before the conference. I sent out a portion of my novel to be considered for one of the coveted seats at the retreat. To my amazement, I was chosen. Immediately doubt set in. Would I ever get over the feeling of not being good enough?

———

The plane is landing. It's not soon enough to suit me. My seatmates have been drinking all the way to Maui. A shuttle ride past sugar plantations and residential areas and I arrive at the Outrigger Wailea Resort. A young Hawaiian man slips a flowered lei around my neck, welcomes me to the hotel, and picks up my bags. I'm speechless, in awe of the sheer beauty of the fabulous open-air reception room filled with couches, tables, and wooden rocking chairs facing the ocean on one side and the mountains on the other. I've never seen anything like it, except in the movies. I have two days to enjoy myself and rest up before the retreat, which is to be held at the Grand Wailea, the hotel next door, begins.

In my room, which certainly doesn't disappoint, I can't wait to call Tom. I wish he were here to experience this with me. He answers. "This room has everything," I say, "a refrigerator, a safe, an ironing board and iron, a coffeepot, even a hair dryer. I could live here." He's happy for me, tells me to have a great time and not to worry about anything at home. This is my time, and it may be the only chance I get to come to Hawaii. There's so much I want to do and my free time is short—once the retreat starts, I'll be busy.

The next morning, the island still cloaked in darkness, I board a busload full of tourists bound for the summit of Haleakala, a dormant volcano ten thousand feet above sea level, to watch the sunrise from above the clouds. We've been told to dress warm. By the time we reach the top, I understand why. The sweatshirt and jacket I brought aren't enough. Others are wearing stocking caps, gloves, and winter outerwear. Cold or not, I'm here, and I'm going to see it. Braced against the chill, I follow others to the railing where we will get the best view of the crater. As soon as the sun peeks through, we can see it and I forget how cold I am. It looks like another planet, a mysterious, misty place from a strange world far away.

There is a small shopping area between the two hotels. I spend the afternoon wandering the shops, stopping at the small grocery for food I can keep in my room because the restaurants are terribly expensive, put on my bathing suit, and I'm off to play in the ocean. It's so nice that I wish I hadn't signed up for the all-day tour of Hana tomorrow. I would just as soon stay here. I've already paid for it, so I'm going.

By the end of the next day, I understand why they sell tee shirts in the gift shops that say, "I survived the road to Hana." Exhausted, I fix a sandwich in my room and go to bed early. I want to be at the other hotel first thing in the morning to register for the retreat, pick up my package, figure out where I'm supposed to go and whose class I'll be in. I discover that when they said the Outrigger was next door to the Grand, they meant a half-mile walk on a winding sidewalk between grass lawns and the beach.

It's hot, humid, and windy as I make my way to the Grand Wailea. As impressed as I was with the Outrigger, this place looks like a Polynesian palace. I still can't believe I'm here. After a few minutes in a plush powder room to fix my hair and cool off, I follow signs to the registration area. I'm registered, and there will be a get-acquainted party tonight. I can hardly wait.

Dressed in white knee-length shorts and a striped top, I begin the trek back to the Grand. I wonder if it was the brightest idea to stay next door. I will save a lot on the room, but will be doing a lot of walking. If I get to attend next year, I'll stay at the big hotel. The party is located on the lower-level patio, an open-air place with tiki torches, an enormous waterfall and pool, tables, and a bar. As soon as I walk in, I realize it's a cocktail party. It doesn't take me long to figure out the lay of the land. Whereas the brochure said we new writers would be rubbing elbows with agents, editors, and best-selling authors, it is obvious to me that that's not what's happening here.

Within an hour, I'm back in my room, making a call to AA. I'm put on hold. No one comes back on the line. I call again. I get a voice mail and reluctantly leave a message. I call Tom. "I want to come home," I say, and tell him about the party, another place I didn't fit in, where I felt like a fish out of water. "I can't do this," I continue. "I don't know why I thought I could. I can't even get hold of anyone in AA."

When I pause to sob into the phone, Tom says, "Give it a couple more days. If you don't like the retreat, you don't have to go. You can go lay by the pool for the next week, or go exploring. I know there is AA there . . . those people are everywhere." I laugh in spite of myself. Feeling better, I hang up and call Donna, my best girlfriend in Yarnell, who's been sober longer than I. After sharing my experiences so far, I tell her I haven't been able to talk to anyone in the program. She says, "Maybe you ought to pray about it."

19

Serendipity

IT'S A NEW DAY. I HAVE A NEW ATTITUDE. Putting my drama queen meltdown of yesterday behind me, I revel in the glorious morning as I saunter along the narrow sidewalk to the Grand. My first class that will teach me to be a better writer. Stopped on an arched wooden bridge over a koi pond that surrounds a stained glass church on three sides, I bow my head and thank God for all that I've been given, for allowing me to be in this wondrous place, and promise that I will give it all I've got.

Although no one from AA returned my call, I reminded myself what Donna always said about it. "The people aren't the program. You know the program, and sometimes it will just be you, God, and the principles of Alcoholics Anonymous." My program tells me that upon arising, I am to turn my will and life over to this God of my understanding, and if I am truly able to do that, whatever happens that day will be for my best. I am always enough. It doesn't matter that I don't look like others, dress in fashion, or that I'm not as well-published or as smart—it's not a competition. For the first time in my life, I'm comfortable in my own skin, and nothing outside me should affect that.

I keep those things in mind as I ready myself for the day ahead. I will be who I am: a short, dark-complexioned woman with a brown mohawk, wearing a summer top and pair of loose-fitting bibbed overalls and sandals. For me, there is nothing worse than trying to be something I'm not. I tried that for many years, and it never worked.

It's quiet. Not many people are wandering around this early in the morning. As I make my way to the coffee shop, I admire the way the building is set up, the enormous statues of plump Hawaiian men and women lolling about, brass railings everywhere. I wonder how they keep it clean. With all the open-air restaurants, bars, and reception areas, it must be difficult. Then there are the birds. They are everywhere, fly right down on the tables while people are eating, begging for crumbs. If this place were in Arizona, it would be constantly covered in dust.

Coffee and a danish in hand, I make my way down a winding wooden staircase that reminds me of something from the Swiss Family Robinson's tree house to the lower level and meeting rooms. The classroom I've been assigned is at the end, next to a waterfall and stream filled with colorful fish. I pull a chair next to the water, glory in all the greenery and flowers around me, savor each bite of the pastry, drink the hot Kona coffee, close my eyes, and go into deep meditation. I picture myself walking down a long hallway with many doors on each side. As I come to each door, it opens, allowing all the wonders of life to be within my grasp.

The sound of voices brings me back to my surroundings. I love to watch people, be a fly on the wall listening in on their conversations. I read that listening will help me write dialogue better . . . besides, I'm a bit nosey. I am absolutely fascinated with the human condition: who people are, what brought them to that point, how they think, and why. I suppose it's because I've had to do so much self-searching over the years.

Six hours later, I am walking back to my hotel. My thoughts rest on the homework assignment our teacher Don McQuinn, a best-selling science fiction author, handed out. Suddenly I hear a voice say, "I wish I'd brought my bibs." I turn to see a woman standing in front of one of the thatched coffee huts near the beach. Surely not. She is wearing a tee shirt with an AA logo and the slogan EASY DOES IT emblazoned across the chest. I approach and say, "Are you a friend of Bill W.?" That's AA code for use when we are in a public place. She smiles, makes a sweeping gesture with her hand, and says, "We all are." There are three other people sitting at a table behind her, drinking coffee. Within minutes, that strange instant bond we friends of Bill W. have has us talking like old friends.

I'm sweaty but thrilled by the time I reach my room. I'm going to a meeting with the two married couples tonight. What a day it has been. I found a common bond with the nine others I'll be attending class with each day. It's a wonderfully diverse group, both ethnically and as writers, although we are all writing fiction, or at least attempting to do so. Mr. McQuinn is an older man, tall and broad-shouldered, with thick white hair and bushy eyebrows that sweep up, giving him the appearance of a wizard. He impressed me with his years of knowledge of the writing and publishing business. He really wants us to learn, to do well with our projects. I like him and look forward to the week ahead. I have to call Tom and Donna to share my good news of the day.

———

It's Labor Day Monday, and I'm on the plane winging my way back to Arizona. I want to sleep, but my mind is too full with the glorious experiences of the past twelve days. Leaving the island was surreal, like waking up from one of the best dreams I ever had. I not only learned a tremendous amount from Don McQuinn; I made a new friend. When I discovered him sitting in front of the meeting room early one morning, we began to talk, and afterwards it became our habit to spend that time together before the others arrived. Once, toward the end of the week, Don said, "Barb, there are a lot of good writers here. Some of them will be better than you, some not as good, but you're going to make it because you're a pit bull."

The meetings I attended at sunset at a pavilion on the beach ruined me for church basements, old schoolrooms, and meeting halls. At the second meeting I attended in Hawaii with my new AA friends, I was asked to be the speaker. Perched on the top of a picnic table, I shared my story with a group of about thirty people. Halfway through my story, much of which revolved around the deaths of my children and the pain I carried with me so long, I noticed a young man weeping. Afterwards, he stepped up to me, wrapped his arms around me, hugged me tightly, and whispered in my ear, "I know God sent you here for me." On the ride home, the couple I rode with—who lived in Maui a portion of the year—told me that the young man and his wife had recently lost a child, and he hadn't been able to put any sober time together since. At that moment, I knew exactly what this trip to Maui was about. The writers retreat and the conference were simply the catalysts.

All the way home from the airport in Phoenix, I can't stop talking, sharing my experiences with Tom. "After that meeting, with the guy in such terrible turmoil," I say, "I stopped worrying about anything else. I realized whatever I got from the writers thing was gravy, so I could relax and enjoy myself, and I did." Even though I discovered I wasn't a very good fiction writer, Don and others in my group taught me what it meant to find my voice in writing. It will take me in an entirely different direction.

I am not putting words on paper now, but writing in my head. With the cooler weather, Tom and I have been doing a lot of hiking, finding new paths, new mountain areas to climb, and have even ferreted out ancient boulders covered in petro-glyphs. Having studied the symbols of rune stones and tarot cards for many years, I'm fascinated by the crude drawings etched into stone that have been there for centuries. They speak to me. I begin to research the symbols, ask around town where others have seen them. It's an exciting adventure going out to the desert, into the mountains, hunting for the treasure that is knowledge of the past. For the first time in a long time, I bring my tarot cards out to study them.

20

In the Cards

IN FLORIDA, YEARS AGO, during my brief marriage to my fourth husband, I had a tarot reading from a woman I'd never met before. I was stunned at how dead-on she was about me and about my future. Intrigued, I inquired about how she learned to read cards. "Books," she said. I can read books. She went on to tell me that she believed everyone had the ability to predict their own future, that the cards are simply a tool. I bought a tarot card kit, studied the meanings for over two years, and began reading, amazed at how accurate the cards could be.

Years later, after reading for hundreds of people and using my cards for everything from meeting men to abusing those I didn't like when I was drinking, karma came back to bite me in the ass. My friend Rita showed up one day and asked for a reading with the death house. Although I'd studied the various layouts for readings, I rarely did an astrological layout with the cards because it was the only one that had a place for serious illness and death. I'd seen enough death to last me a lifetime and simply didn't want to see it in someone else's cards. Rita said she was experiencing an ominous feeling that something bad was going to happen, and she begged me to read her cards. If I hadn't known her so well, I would have refused. I laid the cards out. In the death house fell a light-haired, light-eyed child. The news would come from a brown-haired, brown-eyed man from a distance. My friend was convinced it was her sister's child. They were about to embark on a cross-country move.

Sure enough, less than a month later, the dreaded phone call came. It was from a brown-haired, brown-eyed man, calling from a distance away. My brother! The child who died was my blond-haired, blue-eyed son. My brother called Rita because I didn't have a telephone. She couldn't bear to tell me, so she called Tom, who drove to Sullivan, knocked on the door, and delivered the blow that nearly killed me—and ended my card reading for years.

The self-centered, egotistical fool that I was, I thought that when Jon started having problems and behaving badly, I could handle him. I'd studied psychology all those years in college, been through therapy myself, and knew all the answers, or so I thought. Of course, knowing the answers and applying them to my own life were two entirely different matters. It was one of those do as I say, not as I do situations.

At age 13, Jon began to ask questions about his father. I'd lied to him for years, telling him his father left us and didn't want us. In truth, it wasn't Jon he didn't want. When I divorced Jon's father, I had child support and alimony put in the papers, but told his dad that if he never bothered us or tried to contact us, I would never ask him for a penny of it. He didn't, and I didn't. I continued to lie. Jon kept asking questions.

Offended that he wanted to find his father after I'd taken care of him alone all those years, I argued with Jon. I told him I'd try to locate his dad, and every time he asked, I told him I had some feelers out—another lie.

Like me, Jon turned to drugs and alcohol. I couldn't believe that after all he'd seen me go through, he would do that himself. However, I had watched my mother drink and drug herself right into the grave and did the same thing. Jon became sullen and angry, no longer satisfied with my explanations about not being able to find his dad. Still, I didn't get him the help that might have saved his life.

By age 15, Jon was out of control and decided to take matters into his own hands. He stole a car with the idea of going to Arizona and finding his dad himself. He got caught by the cops. Tom's attorney cut him a deal. If he agreed to probation and a long-term treatment facility, there wouldn't be any jail time. He accepted. Sadly, I packed his clothes and dropped him off in Springfield at Gateway, the treatment center okayed by the judge. The judge told him that if he left, the original charge of car theft would be reinstated and he'd do his time in jail.

Within a couple of weeks at Gateway, Jon broke his leg playing basketball. As soon as the cast was removed, he disappeared. He got a message to me to call him at an unfamiliar number. Using a pay phone, I punched in the number, sure I could talk him into returning to the treatment center. He'd hitchhiked to Florida, where he had some friends. As soon as I knew where he was, I should have told the police, but I didn't. He said he was going to Arizona. Fearful about him hitching rides with strangers, I asked him to wait until I could make some arrangements. After begging money from Tom, I called my brother. Jon was to take a bus to Phoenix and stay with him.

He made it to my brother's house and begged me to come to Arizona. He said we could start over. Everything in me wanted to go, to be with him, but for the first time, I thought I would do the right thing and try to act like a real parent. I told myself if I went, if I gave in to him, I would be following him forever—and sooner or later he'd get caught and we'd both go to jail. I refused. That was the day I uttered that prayer, asked God to take care of him. Shortly after, I read the cards for my friend. Not long after that, Jon was dead. The cards wrapped in cloth, I placed them in a box and put them in the top of the closet. I never wanted to look at them again.

———

Tom finds me sitting at the table, shuffling my tarot cards. Surprised, he says, "What are you doing?" What am I doing? What am I thinking? Can I really do it? "What if," I say, "I do a fortune-telling kit using petroglyphs?"

21

Life

IT'S AN UNSEASONABLY WARM FEBRUARY AFTERNOON in 2006 when we drive into the parking lot of the small animal hospital. Sammi, our Italian greyhound, on a leash, we walk the hilly area specified for dogs to relieve themselves. Business completed, we start toward the building. I feel my feet slipping. I lose control and fall on some loose rocks. The loop of the leash drops to the ground. Sammi's loose. Frightened, she runs toward the highway. Jumping up and putting the pain in my back aside, I chase her. Tom heads her off in the parking lot. He hands me the leash. Heart pounding, I hold her close, thinking of what might have happened.

Sammi hasn't been acting like herself. Recently, when we pick her up, she squeals as if in pain. We're here to get her checked out. In the waiting room, after the X-rays, we wait. Wrapped in her favorite blanket, Sammi looks at me with her big, brown, trusting eyes, and I pet her back to assure her that everything will be all right. I know she's old, but she's healthy. I pull her close to my chest.

We're called back into the exam room. The vet says she's got a growth on her spleen. It must be removed. Reluctantly, I hand Sammi over. Even though the vet says it will be a while, that Tom and I should go get something to eat, I can't leave . . . to abandon my beloved dog in a strange place alone. Back in the waiting room, Tom and I sit in adjoining leather chairs. Tom's hand covers mine. He squeezes. He can say more with the touch of his hand than anyone ever conveyed to me in words.

In all of my life, I've never had another person who I knew was there for me no matter what. Tom has been there through so much and never questioned, blamed, or shamed me. When I got in trouble, made the call, he always came through—paying for my divorces, bailing me out financially, giving me cars, helping with Jon, paying for lawyers. I jumped from one bad situation to another, always searching for that elusive something that would make me happy. And though I had many brief encounters that I called marriage, Tom never married, insisting that we would end up together one day.

We've been married for over twenty years, which is a miracle considering my track record. I'm not sure why, but in the throes of my drinking and drug use, my solutions consisted of moving, changing jobs, and getting married. I only stayed in new places for a short time for fear that others would figure out the truth of who I was. I couldn't hold jobs any length of time because I was always on the run. And marriages . . . well, one of us always sobered up, reality hit, and at the first sign of trouble, I was planning my escape. I called them adventures, but they were disasters. I lived in a state of excited misery for years.

By the time I dragged myself into the first 12-step meeting, I was tired—tired of running, tired of living the way I did, tired of dreading every new sunrise. I wanted to stop, to rest, to find a moment's peace. It took finding peace while living in the garage, staying sober, working my steps, and not asking anyone else to bail me out of trouble before I was ready for an honest, lasting relationship. It took opening myself to a Higher Power to understand what it means to love and be loved, to feel worthy of a good life.

I had an epiphany at a 12-step meeting for women many years ago. New to sobriety, I sat through it listening to other women talk about their devastations over husbands cheating, leaving them alone, driving them to drink. I recall thinking, what a bunch of whiners. I got divorced all the time. What was the big deal? It didn't dawn on me until much later that they actually loved their husbands. I kept marrying men I didn't even like that much so that when it ended I wouldn't feel the way those ladies did. I wasn't willing to put my heart on the line, to risk the pain. That's probably why I didn't marry Tom. I was in love with him. He could hurt me.

I look over at Tom. He's worried too. Without any children or grandchildren, our dogs fill a hole in our lives. As a child, my best friend was a dog: Pedro, the tough little Manchester terrier. He was whom I went to with my secrets, my fears, my tears. When my children died, dogs filled my empty arms that ached to hold a baby. Georgie, who's at home waiting for us, saw me through the loss of my son's dog, Angel. Sammi, who's in surgery now, helped me get through the suffering caused by being housebound with Graves' disease for so long.

The vet is coming toward us. I don't like the look on his face. Breath held in, I stand. Tom puts his arm around my waist. All day I've been trying to use the eleventh step . . . praying "only" for God's will and the power to carry it out. The vet motions us to follow him into another room. As we walk in, I look over his shoulder through a glass barrier. Sammi is laid out on an operating table, still under the anesthetic. The vet says, "Sammi has cancer. It has metastasized. I can bring her back if you want, but the kindest thing you can do now is let her go."

An old, familiar knot begins to form in my gut. Unable to speak, I nod. He says, "I'll take care of it and get her ready if you want to say good-bye." Pictures of my babies dead in my arms flood my mind. I can't do it. I shake my head, look to Tom who I know is as upset as I am, and, as always, he knows what I need. I have to get out of here. He ushers me out the door. By the time we reach the car, I'm convulsing in pain, strange sounds coming from deep inside me, tears flowing unchecked down my face. He wraps me in a gentle embrace.

My eyes red and swollen and the end of my nose raw from wiping at it with a paper towel by the time we get home, I wonder if I have enough left in me to walk up the hill to the house. Tom helps me. Inside, I'm reminded of the day I learned of Jon's death as I weep into Georgie's soft fur.

Something's wrong with Tom. I don't think I've ever seen that look on his face. He slams out the door. I follow. He says, "He should have told us. I didn't even get to hold her before he took her. I just thought it was some little operation. He shouldn't have taken us back there . . . you know, where we could see her laying there." I've never seen him so angry.

Quickly, I realize that because he can't deal with the pain of loss, he's gone directly to anger and is placing blame on the vet. I say, "It wasn't his fault. He tried to save her. He might have handled it better, but it is what it is." Tom begins to break down. I wrap my arms around him as he had with me earlier, and we mourn together. This is what a real marriage is about—being there for each other through whatever life throws at us. We'd made it through my disease, Tom's bout with prostate cancer, the loss of two brothers-in-law as well as Tom's brother and sister, and we'd make it through this. "We still have Georgie," I say, "and she needs us." I glance at her dancing around our feet, glad we're home, and know that soon we'll be going through another loss. She's nearly 20 years old.

I bring the eleventh step to mind as I weep softly into my pillow, missing the feel of Sammi curled up next to me. I know that I must keep this conscious contact with the God of my understanding or I will be swallowed up by the pain of Sammi's loss and of the past. I can't allow myself to go backward. I'll get up and write in the morning, as I do each morning. I'm working under a deadline on my new book.

Thinking of the new project, an inspirational book based on the Serenity Prayer, makes me remember all the good things in my life. Tom and I have had quite a run for the past twenty-one years. Considering the kind of lives we led—drinking, screwing around, doing sometimes unspeakable things—I am in awe of the life we've had together. I never knew it could be like this. With Tom's help, I realized my dream of becoming a costumer, ran a successful business before I got sick, and now he's happily retired and I'm an author. To date, in addition to my costume books and the fortune-telling kit, I have three inspirational books published and am about to finish another. But what I count as the greatest achievement in my life is that I've become a genuinely decent person, a trusted friend to many, and a devoted wife, thanks to the help of a program, people who cared for me when I wasn't capable of caring for myself, and divine intervention. A person simply can't get to where I am, from where I started, without divine intervention.

Late into the night, I pace the floor. I smoke. I cry. I try to obliterate the image of Sammi lying on that cold metal table, her side cut open. When I begin to feel a twinge of pain in my right side and back, I take to my bed. Totally exhausted, I sleep, only to awaken a few hours later in agony. Every time I move, sharp pains slice through my side and back. It must have been the fall. After a hot tub soak and some arthritis cream rubbed into the sore areas, I'll be fine.

Unable to return to sleep, I sit down at my desk to work on the book. Within seconds, doubled over in misery, I stand. I need to walk it off, to loosen up, but each step I take makes it worse. Standing in the middle of my kitchen floor, questions float into my mind. Why me? Why now? Aren't I in enough pain already? What the hell is happening? I've been good. I'm sober, working the program, pray every day, help others, and try to be the best person I can be. "Why?" I scream at God. As soon as I hear myself, I stop. What am I doing? I'd heard it around the meetings so many times: drunk or sober, life keeps happening. It's what we do with what happens that's important. For those of us who have chosen to live a spiritually based life, God is everything, or God is nothing.

It has been easy living a spiritually based life over the past ten years, when everything was going my way. How many times have I said to people in meetings, "If you believe one thing in your life happened for a reason, then you must believe all things happen for a reason. You don't get to pick and choose"? How easily those words came out of my mouth. Do I really believe it?

22

The Challenge

SOOTHING MUSIC WAFTS SOFTLY THROUGH A ROOM painted in soft shades of green, peaceful artwork adorning each wall. I'm lying on a padded table in the center of the room with skinny needles protruding from my ankles, wrists and hands, side, and the top of my head. This woman is good. She poked those needles right into my skin without inflicting any pain. I'm still amazed I'm here, considering my great fear of needles.

Since, as a child, I was forced to go to a ham-fisted ex-army dentist friend of my stepfather, the thought of needles evokes fear and pain. I can see the dentist's hairy hand coming toward my face, holding a needle so large it looks like it could go all the way through my head. He hurt me more times than I care to remember. I don't know if my bad teeth were genetic or if what he did to me all those years didn't work, but I ended up with false teeth by the time I turned 17. The one thing he did do for me was to instill in me such a fear of needles that he inadvertently kept me from becoming a heroin addict. God knows the people I ran around with over the years gave me every opportunity.

"Please, let this help," I whisper to God. It had been a long, painful year since Sammi's death. At first I stayed in bed, living in fear of moving because I knew I would suffer sharp, debilitating pains that felt like someone had shoved a hot poker through my side. Every time I sat up it felt like a big fiery ball had lodged itself beneath my rib cage, which would send me reeling to a prone position, holding my breath until the pain passed. I wondered if I had one of those giant tumors growing inside me like people I'd seen on television. I knew anything that hurt that bad had to be something terrible. The worst part of lying around day by day was the silence, all that time to think. Thoughts began to creep into my mind, angry, resentful thoughts that brought me feelings of self-pity and finally depression—all things an addict in recovery can ill afford. It didn't matter that I'd been sober and drug-free all those years because at the end of the day, I was still an addict. I knew what would take the pain away, at least for a while.

One afternoon, as I wallowed in my misery, both physical and mental, another thought came to mind: you can live in the problem or live in the solution . . . it's entirely up to you. I'd heard it said many times in meetings, but had never needed to hear it as profoundly as I did at that moment. Jack used to say that attending meetings was like making payments on an insurance policy. I may not need something I hear at a meeting for a week, a year, or ten years, but when I need it, it'll be there. Then he would add, "Of course, if you don't show up, you may miss hearing the very thing that can save your ass down the road, and your policy could lapse." I'd seen it time and again— people with years in sobriety who suffered a trauma and went back out.

When the fear of relapse became bigger than the fear of the pain, I got on my feet, determined not to let it happen to me. I talked to Tom about my decision. I knew that whatever choice I made, he would go along with it. One of the things I loved most about him was that he treated me like an equal with the ability to know what was best for myself. That was certainly something I'd never experienced in a relationship before. I said, "We're going to have to change some things around." The pain lessened when I was standing or lying down, so we'd have to set the household up differently, just as a person in a wheelchair had to do.

The transition began. Tom moved a waist-high table into the corner of the kitchen and placed my typewriter atop it so I could stand to write. He removed my favorite chair, the one that hung from a beam that separated the kitchen from the dining area, and set up an outside lounge chair instead so I could lie back to watch my television. To eat, I'd stand at the bar. Tom carried a thick blanket and pillow down the hill to the car and arranged it in the backseat as a bed for when I was forced to ride somewhere. It felt good to get into action. That feeling was short-lived when I knew the next phase was at hand: calling the doctor.

After all I'd gone through with my Graves' disease, the mere thought of going back to a doctor sent a shudder through my spine. For six months, truly believing that death hung over my head, I'd made the rounds to one specialist after another. They poked, prodded, and ran tests, but I continued to get worse. Some doctors acted as if it was all in my head, others shook their heads and said, "I just don't know." When I nearly died, eventually ending up in the emergency room where I was finally diagnosed, I had to deal with many doctors who'd never had a Graves' disease patient. They were not terribly sure of what to do with me. I got sick of hearing things like, "let's try this."

I stood staring at the telephone for long moments, telling myself that it had to be done and assuring myself that to base the present on the past did no good. I made the call, and by the afternoon I was standing in a crowded emergency room in Sun City, waiting to be seen. Hours later, it began: doctor after doctor guessing what they thought might be wrong with me, grueling tests that showed nothing, pills that caused hives, itching, some that made me fall down, others that caused bleeding and low blood pressure, but nothing that helped.

My situation was similar to before, but I was different. No matter how bad the pain, I rose in the morning, got on my knees to pray—not for the pain to be taken away, but for God's will for me and the power to carry it out. I went to my typewriter each morning to write, even if a few sentences was the best I could do. I did housework that didn't require much bending and allowed Tom to do those things that caused me pain. I climbed in the backseat of the car. Tom drove me to meetings where I stood in the back of the room for an hour. I participated and continued to sponsor others, though I had to do much of it over the phone. I stopped focusing on what I couldn't do, instead concentrating on what was possible. At the end of each day, lying in my bed, I thanked God for my life, my husband, Georgie, clean sheets, a warm, safe place to sleep, the ability to stand, and so much more. They weren't simply words. I really meant it. I'd finally come to understand what step 12 meant when it said to use the program in all my affairs.

———

Kristina, the thin, attractive blond acupuncturist, is removing the needles. She sits on a stool next to the table and says, "The Asians believe that we store our pain and loss in the liver. Maybe you did that after your little dog died, and it triggered all those losses from the past." An interesting concept. I figured I'd resolved all those issues as much as a person can resolve the death of children. A brown bottle of homeopathic drops and an appointment card in my hand, I lie down in the backseat of the car, mulling over what she'd said. If it's true, what's to be done?

I'd heard there is no problem, large or small, that can't be resolved by taking it through the steps. Back to basics. Standing at the bar, pen in hand, I begin to write: "I am powerless over the pain of loss, and it has made my life unmanageable. I believe that a God of my understanding can help me. I will turn this over to God, and accept that the outcome is not up to me but will always be for my best in the long run." That wasn't so hard. Next is my fearless moral inventory. I did that years ago. What if I didn't do enough? I know I had a hard time writing about my part in the kids' deaths because I didn't really think I had much responsibility for something so out of my control. Did I skim over that part of my life? Was I fearless? Did I search the deepest part of my soul, looking for the truth of my part in things?

During my first fourth and fifth steps, I'd admitted that I liked being pregnant because it made me feel special—I wanted to make my husband at the time love me; plus, he hardly ever hit me when I was carrying his child. Even though the doctors told me that I would have trouble carrying a baby to term after Jon tore me up so bad, we didn't use protection, and I got pregnant at the drop of a hat. I understood that I thrived on the attention I got when the babies died and that I used their deaths to excuse my addictive behavior.

Perhaps now I need to go deeper, back to that dark place where all my secrets hid out for so many years. Had I simply cracked the door before, let out what I could handle, and then closed it quickly for fear of the shame and guilt I'd have to deal with if I shined a light on the whole truth? After a restless night—between the pain and the questions whirling through

If I Die Before I Wake

my mind, I am out of bed before the sun rises—I get on my knees and ask for the strength to do what has to be done. Lying on the lounge chair in the middle of the kitchen, embracing the quiet morning, I close my eyes and imagine I'm walking down that long hallway full of doors. This time, instead of all the doors opening, I move toward a door at the end of the hallway. I turn the knob. It's locked. I pull a huge skeleton key off a nail nearby, but hesitate before I stick it in the keyhole. Imagining a white light surrounding me, the key pushed into the hole, I turn it slowly.

My eyes snap open. Quickly, I'm on my feet, doubled over in pain. Was I meditating, or did I fall asleep? Slowly, I straighten up and glance at the clock on the stove. Two hours have passed. I must have gone to sleep. I can rarely recall having a dream that real, with such clarity. When the door creaked open, what was behind it looked like a scene from a horror show: a veil of cobwebs clinging to my skin and hair, spiders hanging by a thread, pitch-black darkness. Like a drum, I heard each beat of my heart in my ears. Sweat trickled down my spine. The white light I'd imagined around myself began to fade. The urge to run nearly overwhelmed me. I stood still, and said, "As I walk through the valley of the shadow of death, I will fear no evil."

Bolstered by my belief that I was not alone, I stepped forward. Dark figures moved in the shadows, whispering words I couldn't understand. I knew they were watching me, talking about me. I wondered if they were the black ghosts with white eyes who haunted my dreams as a child. The sound of someone sobbing caught my attention. I moved toward it. A light flashed over a woman lying in a hospital bed, her face pushed into a pillow, weeping. I moved closer. It was me.

As if I'd flipped a switch on a strobe light, I watched in horror as the moments of my life were highlighted, one after another. I wanted to run, tried to look away. I willed my legs to move. Nothing happened. Babies in coffins, my mother holding a gun, Jon laid out in the morgue, dead dogs, myself beat up, beat down, strapped to a bed with a big rubber thing crammed into my mouth while a doctor shoots me through with electricity. The actions that led up to each event appeared and disappeared like a slide show. The last thought I had was that I'd died, and the time had come to face the truth. Naked and alone, with no one else to blame and nowhere to hide, I would be accountable for every thought and action.

Days pass by as I go about the business of living, but ever in the back of my mind is the memory of that dream. It reminds me of a time in therapy when the therapist hypnotized me in an attempt to help me regain some of the memories lost through childhood trauma, and later, months of shock therapy in the mental hospital. A doctor had once told me that as time went on, I would recall those things that my mind could handle remembering. I didn't expect it to happen this late in my life, or all at once. I tell myself it was just a disturbing dream, but wonder why it lives in my mind with such clarity.

23

Truth or Consequences

GEORGIE'S DEAD. SHE HAD A STROKE. In the early morning hours as I sat at my typewriter, thrilled to be pain-free, I heard her yelp. She fell from the chair near where I work. We rushed her to the vet, but it was too late. Logically, I know she was old, that she'd had over twenty wonderful years, but it doesn't diminish the anguish—that familiar burning knot that forms in the belly and reminds me of all the losses in my life. The emptiness in the house is nothing compared to the emptiness in my heart.

As much as I hate the person I've been in the past and regret what I did to cope with my losses, I know that in an instant I can revert backward, indulge the fleeting temptation of a shot of whiskey or a pill to take the edge off. My mind tries to trick me, telling me I've been sober all these years, that I could handle one drink, a couple pills—just enough to get me through the moment. But I know me—one drink, one pill, and I'm off and running again. Will addiction ever leave me completely?

I need to do something physical. Years ago, in early recovery, on a particularly bad day when I fought the urge to drink moment by moment, I called a woman I'd met at a meeting. Expecting a profound solution for my situation, she surprised me when she said, "Have you mopped your floors?" What? Then she said, "Mop your floors, and call me back." I scrubbed the concrete floors of the garage with a brush and called her back. She said, "Have you defrosted your refrigerator?" I told her I hadn't. She said, "Do that, and call me back." All day she gave me chores to do until by the end of the day, sore and exhausted, I didn't have the energy or inclination left to drink.

Outside there's a project I haven't been able to finish. Gathering up the wheelbarrow full of quartz rocks Tom and I have been picking up at the old mine sites, I use a sledgehammer to break up the larger rocks to the desired size I need to cover the old chimney at the side of the house. Hours later, after soaking in a bath, I'm feeling better. Slipping between the sheets, still missing Georgie next to me, I thank God for everything I can think of and try to picture my little dog in a field of flowers, running and playing with my son and my other dogs.

Like something out of a Stephen King movie, I enter the realm of my nightmare again. Without walking, I move toward that same door . . . the one at the end of the hall, the one that scares me. It's filled with the bodies of the dead. I fight back. My legs won't move. "No! No! No!" I scream. A voice, saying gentle words, wakes me. It's Tom. What am I doing in the hallway? Tom leads me back to bed. I can't believe I walked in my sleep. I haven't done that in a long time. Although it was a common occurrence in my childhood, the last time I did it happened after we moved to Arizona and my dad made his first visit. The night before he arrived, Tom found me wandering the house in the middle of the night, eyes wide open, completely unconscious.

In the morning, having slept through the remainder of the night, I swing my legs over the side of the bed. As quickly as I put weight on my legs, an excruciating pain travels through my side, into my back, and down my hip and leg. I fall back onto the bed. What have I done to myself this time? It crosses my mind that it might not be all physical. Like most addicts, I have a tendency toward self-sabotage when things are going well. In the meetings it's called keeping the drama alive.

Things had been going well for a while. After a number of sessions with the acupuncturist, the pain went away. Filled with gratitude for the ability to sit down, to ride in the car, to do my own housework, I pushed aside thoughts that perhaps I hadn't resolved everything from my past. Occasionally, Kristina's words passed through my mind, but I told myself it was silly. I'd done the work, faced my part in things, and it was time to let it go.

I overdid it yesterday. I need to walk it off. Carefully, I ease onto my feet, suffering with each step I take toward the bathroom. For days, I limp around the house, unable to sit, stand, or lie down comfortably. I finally give in and call the doctor. The neurologist thinks I have shingles inside my body. I've heard of shingles going in after a breakout, but I've never had a breakout. The gastric doctor says it's my gallbladder and quickly sucks that baby out of me. The back surgeon wants to do surgery to remove some calcification between two of my discs. I allow him to cut the middle of my back open and remove the offending piece. It works on the pain in my hip and leg. I can stand and walk again. However, the horrific pain in my side remains with no clear cause.

Frustrated by the situation, I need to talk to someone in the program—someone who understands. I call an old friend. I pour out all that's happened recently; Kristina's idea, the nightmares, the sleepwalking. The woman on the phone, who had known me for most of my sobriety, says, "When you did your fourth and fifth steps, did you tell it all, you know, leaving nothing out?" I am silent for a long moment. She says, "I don't know if it has anything to do with the physical stuff, but you know that when you have these dreams and start walking in your sleep again, something is wrong. Only you can figure it out."

Unhappy with the conversation, I make several more calls to people who don't know me quite so well, seeking different answers to the same questions. No one can reassure me that I'm okay, that I've done all I can. Somewhere where the brutal truth lives, I know what I've done, what I left out when I worked the fourth and fifth steps. I think I've always known, but refused to admit it. How many times have I said, "If you work a thorough fourth and fifth step, leaving nothing out, and stick with the maintenance steps, you should never have to do them again." Others argued with me from time to time, convinced I shouldn't be spouting those words around new people, but my pride wouldn't let me back down.

How humiliating it will be to admit I've been wrong all these years. I don't want to do it, to open that door again, to delve deeper into my memories, to tell another person the awful things I've done and how they led to the deaths of my children. But I've got to do something. I can't live with the nightmares anymore. Before, when they had gotten so bad I became afraid to go to sleep, I had started drinking. This time, I have to own up to the "exact" nature of my wrongs, because I know that's where I failed the first time.

I had chosen Jack, my first sponsor and friend, to be the human being with whom I purged my soul. I didn't lie. I didn't soft-pedal what I'd done, simply omitting my selfish, shameful behavior during my pregnancies, but I did play with words, saying, "I didn't drink when I was pregnant." The ugly truth is that I didn't drink whiskey, but I had discovered other numbing substances like cough syrup, mouthwash, pills I pilfered from other people's medicine cabinets, and over-the-counter products. Sometimes I hadn't even been sure what I was putting in my mouth, and I had never considered what it might be doing to my babies.

I had made myself sound like the victim because I was living with a brutal man, but it had been my children who were the victims. I had always told myself I didn't have choices. My husband had wanted babies. If I gave him babies maybe he would love me and stop hitting me. Even when I had attempted to make amends to my dead babies—dead because they were born too early and had serious health problems, I had refused to admit the truth. Their deaths were a direct result of my actions. I couldn't tell Jack, or anyone else, that I had killed my children.

Now my actions have come home to roost, are stealing my peace, perhaps affecting me physically. I must tell someone, say it out loud, or what I've done will continue to grow like a cancer in my mind. Nervous but determined, I wait for my friend, the one who has known me well for so many years, who never lets me get away with anything, to answer my call. I nearly lose my courage when I hear her voice. The thing is, I like being well-thought-of in my AA circle, considered a person who has overcome so much trauma and tragedy and come out the better for it. False pride, my mind screams. What will she think of me after I divulge my sick secrets after all these years?

When she asks me how I'm doing, I fight the urge to tell her I'm fine and let it go at that. "Not so great," I say. "Do you have time to hear a mini fifth step?" There's a moment of silence before she responds in the positive. I begin. Sharing recent events, my health problem, Kristina's words, the nightmares, I explain that I've had an epiphany about having withheld information during my first fifth step. How often I've heard her say that recovery is like peeling an onion, each layer getting closer to the core. "The truth is," I say, "I didn't just realize I didn't tell it all. I've known it all along. I haven't had the courage to do it."

"Why?"

"With every other disgusting thing I've done in my life, it's the most shameful." Between having heard my story numerous times in AA and private conversations we'd had, there wasn't much she didn't know about me. But not this one thing. Discarding the idea of prefacing my confession with explanations and excuses, I say, "I killed my kids."

After a pregnant pause, she says, "What does that mean?"

I launch into my story. "I told Jack I didn't drink when I was pregnant, that I tried my best to take care of myself in the face of insurmountable odds. That wasn't true. The truth is that I didn't drink whiskey, beer, or wine, but searched for anything else that contained alcohol. If it wasn't too terrible-tasting, I drank it." I went on, telling her of the instances when I stole pills from my mother's medicine cabinet, raided my in-laws' stash of pills. Anytime my husband and I visited friends, I spent time in the bathroom going through their medications, slipping pills into my purse to take later. "My life was shit, but I didn't have any right to abuse my children . . . even if they weren't born yet."

She's quiet. I can't falter now. "When I was pregnant with my youngest son, the doctor put me on bed rest. He said if I wanted to carry the baby full term, I'd have to stay in bed, eat right, and avoid stress. I agreed. Saying it and doing it were two different things. When left alone, I got up, smoked cigarettes and pot when I could get it, and continued to take stuff that could harm the baby. I don't know if I thought it didn't matter, or if I was so involved with my own pain that I didn't care, but it doesn't matter now. I did it, and when he was born premature with all kinds of health problems, and I watched him fight for every breath he took in his short lifetime, I blamed God and everyone else. I grabbed hold of his death as an excuse to continue my behavior."

"You couldn't do what you didn't know how to do," she responds.

"I've heard that before. In fact, I used it to excuse what I did. But even an animal has better instincts than I had. No, I need to say it. I killed my kids."

"You didn't want to hurt them . . . did you?"

I have to think about that. "I don't know. I don't know what I was thinking, if I was thinking. Apparently, I wasn't thinking about them. All I wanted was to get through the day without hurting, to not have to face my life and the mess I was in."

"I know you made some poor choices."

Poor choices? That's the understatement of the year. "There's more."

Silently, she waits.

"Through it all, I never gave a thought to what Jon was going through. He was a little boy. He needed a mother, not some drunk, witless bitch who couldn't see past her own nose to his pain. You know, by the time he was 5 years old, he was taking care of me. We reversed roles. I robbed him of his childhood. He grew up too fast, and then he became me. I remember something my brother told me after Jon died. He said Jon's biggest problem was that he was too much like me. It's ironic, isn't it? When I was a kid, I used to watch my mother and tell myself

I would never be like her. I ended up just like her in many ways. I wonder if Jon thought the same thing about me?" Fighting the emotional surge building to tears, I tell myself this is not the time for self-pity or recriminations, but the brutal truth.

"Well, since you can't go back and change the past, what are you going to do with it now?"

I haven't thought past saying it out loud to someone. It's difficult to make amends to those who have died. I tried before by praying, by writing letters and burning them. I can't even remember where my babies are buried except that it was in a cemetery off Grand Avenue in Phoenix. At the very least I could stand over Jon's grave and tell myself he could hear my words, understand how much I regretted what I'd done to him. "I don't know yet."

"I know it's not the same thing, but when I couldn't find a way to make amends to my mother for the worry I caused her, I dug out a picture of her, propped it on my desk, and wrote her a letter saying everything I would say to her if she were alive today. Then, I placed the picture and letter in a little box, and put it away."

"Did it work?"

"It did for me."

"Thank you," I say and hang up the receiver. It's worth a try.

24

My Name Is Barb

THE STRANGEST THOUGHTS GO THROUGH MY MIND at the oddest times. At this moment, I can hear old Bob's deep voice saying to me, "When you decide you're just another drunk, that the world doesn't revolve around your ass, you're going to start doing a lot better." I was only a few months sober, and it really pissed me off. Now, it gives me comfort. I hear my name announced.

I step to the podium. It must have been built for a tall person. Moving to the side of it, I scan a sea of faces waiting for me to speak. Clumped together on the right are the young people still in treatment, to the left, a variety of others—workers from the treatment centers, people I've seen in meetings but don't know, a few people I sponsor, and those I call friends. For a small, tourist town, Wickenburg, Arizona has more than its share of treatment facilities. There is certainly a place for everyone, suffering from every imaginable addiction.

There is one person in the audience who needs to hear my story, I tell myself. That's what Jack told me. When I'm asked to speak, I understand that I am being given an opportunity to touch a life in a positive way. "Hi, I'm Barb, and I'm an alcoholic."

"Hi, Barb," the audience responds in unison.

"I was going to say I am a grateful recovering alcoholic, but I remember in my early sobriety I heard someone say that, and it made me want to gag." Laughter fills the room. They know what I'm talking about. "Although I've been sober and straight for a long time, the most important thing is that I haven't had to have a drink or take any other mind-numbing substance today. There was a time when, without hesitation, I would put anything in my mouth that made me feel better. From the first time I stole one of my mother's pills and had my first drink of booze, I knew it was for me. It was the solution to all my problems. I had an absolute affair with alcohol. I loved dirty old bars, dirty old men, beer-drinking music, and oblivion. It worked for me, probably saved my life at times, until it stopped working."

Heads are nodding. "For those of you who don't like to hear a drunkalog, you might as well leave because if you don't know where I've been, you can't understand what it took for me to get where I am today." I pause. No one leaves. "You had your chance," I say, and continue. "I grew up with alcoholics and drug addicts, and everything that went along with that lifestyle. You know what they say . . . alcoholics don't have relationships, they take hostages. I couldn't have felt more like a hostage if they'd blindfolded me, gagged me, and held a gun to my head. The only thing missing was a cigarette dangling from my lips, and I got around to that pretty quickly. That was another great moment in my life: when I first drew that wonderful hot smoke deep in my lungs, nearly choked to death, and thought, I've got to have more of that." Great roars of laughter fill the room.

"If you ever wonder about where it says in the book that we are mentally and bodily different from others, consider those early moments of booze, pills, pot, sex, and other drugs. It didn't matter how much I puked, coughed, tripped—you know, not in a good way—or had other bad experiences, I wanted more. An old friend in the program used to say that if you ate chili and it did that to you, you'd never eat chili again. She wasn't wrong. I was in it for the effect. It didn't take me long to figure out if a little is good, a lot is better.

"As many of you know, I never had one of anything. Early in my sobriety, my sponsor asked me if I had a hobby—besides drinking. The only thing I could think of was marriage. I gave him one of my confused looks. He asked if I collected anything. Finally, I said, 'Wedding rings and divorce papers.' I don't think that's what he was talking about."

I look at my watch. My time is limited. I can't afford to get off on tangents. "Starved for attention, willing to do whatever it took to feel loved, I had actual intercourse for the first time when I was 15 years old. Just once. I got pregnant. That's the way it had been all my life. My brother, who was a year older, got away with everything, and I always got caught. He was the 'good' child, and I was the bad seed. Bad was one of the words used to describe me. There were many more, and none of them good. Let me tell you that when you're told you are a piece of shit loud enough and long enough, you will come to believe you are a piece of shit.

"That's the person I carried into my adulthood, if that's what you would call it. It's been said that if you are an alcoholic, your emotional growth stops when you begin drinking. I believe that's true. When I sobered up, I figure I hit puberty and menopause at the same time. I didn't know whether to grow hair, or shave it off." Again, they laugh. That's what I love about being with other alcoholics and addicts; that sick sense of humor that is lost on normies. These people get me. While in the throes of addictions, addicts tend to laugh when they are sad and cry when they're happy. But, this . . . this is real laughter, coming from a place of understanding.

"My first marriage lasted about four hours. I was eight months pregnant; he married me to keep from going to jail because he was twice my age, and then he left. I had a beautiful, healthy baby boy a month later. Talk about children having children! I didn't have a driver's license, but I thought I could be a mother. Maybe they ought to make us pass a test and get a license before we are allowed to have children. I tried to be a good mother, but didn't have a clue." I feel strong emotions beginning to bubble to the surface. I stop, take a drink of water out of the glass on the podium, and fight the urge to cry.

It's time to say it. I don't know if I can. But it's part of my story. "My next marriage was speed-induced. I woke up in Las Vegas in a strange room with no idea how I got there. You know how it is when you come out of a blackout and you know there's someone next to you in bed, but you're afraid to look. When I looked, all I could see was long blond hair. I thought I was in bed with a woman. However, when he turned over, there was no doubt it was a man—not just a man, but my new husband. We'd been drinking and taking speed for days, got in his girlfriend's car, and drove to Nevada. It probably seemed like a good idea at the time. The sad part is that this marriage lasted longer than any of the others, until now.

"Don't worry, I'm not going to go into detail about all my husbands. We'd be here a very long time. The reason this unholy alliance lasted was because he kept me pregnant, barefoot, and friendless, and beat me up regularly. He wanted babies. We drank and drugged together, until I got pregnant, at which time, I was supposed to take care of myself while he continued his lifestyle."

Here goes . . . my shameful secret. "Our baby girl came early, and every moment of her life was a struggle. She died." A small sob escapes. "I blamed my addicted mother, who was having an affair with my doctor, telling myself that she coerced him into insisting I have a natural birth with my first child, Jon, to teach me a lesson—and that he tore me up so bad that I couldn't carry another baby to term. But the truth was that

I sneaked around, drinking anything I could find with an alcohol content, took other people's pills when I could get my hands on them, and feigned illnesses so I could buy over-the-counter drugs. I never gave a thought to what I was doing to the baby. I blamed my husband because he didn't treat me well, but the truth was that I used to push him to the edge, knowing he would hit me. Isn't that pathetic? I guess I thought if he cared enough to smack me around, it meant he loved me."

The laughter has changed to dead silence. "This would set the tone for many years of my life. My son was born less than a year later, but met the same fate as my daughter. Shortly thereafter, my mom shot herself. Hell, even the doctor committed suicide six months later." I look out at the young people from a treatment center which caters to those under 25. "When I was young, like many of you, instead of ending up in a treatment facility, I ended up in a nuthouse. Believe me when I tell you there are worse places you could be. However, because I nearly ended up in prison for murder, it was the better option. Yes, I planned to kill my abusive husband. He was out drinking. I lay in bed with the biggest butcher knife I could find and waited. I was going to cut him into pieces and cook him in the deep fryer. Oh, I wasn't going to eat him like they did in *Fried Green Tomatoes*." I chuckle. "I might have fed him to some of those snobs at the country club where I worked, who looked down their noses at me. But he didn't come home that night. Instead of committing murder, I took off, dragging my 4-year-old son with me."

Conscious of my time, I speed up the story. I say, "I was 25 years old. I woke up tied hand and foot to a bed, in a white room. My first thought was that this was the cleanest motel I'd ever seen. When I realized I was tied up, I imagined that soon there would be some man walking through the door in leathers, carrying a whip. That should explain where I was in my life. The truth was that I was in a mental hospital. For months, they drugged me, shocked me, and analyzed me, until one day, I got to go home. But I didn't have a home. My son was at my ex-husband's house. That was my third husband, who'd driven to Kentucky to get Jon and I when the man we were traveling with decided he missed his wife and kids and left us stranded."

I forgot something. "My third husband was the result of a drunken temper tantrum. When I ran away from Arizona to Illinois, I met a man. There was always a man. But this one was different. I fell head over heels in love with him. It scared the hell out of me. I did everything I could to sabotage the relationship, finally getting drunk, pissed, and running off with another guy. That showed him! My third marriage was disastrous from day one. But thank God, husband number three had real feelings for me because even after I divorced him, he came and got us when we were stranded. I thought he must be a decent guy, but after I got on my feet with a place of my own, he became a stalker. It wasn't love, but obsession." A shiver tingles my spine at the thought of a scary time in my life, never knowing when, or where, he would show up—or what he might do.

"Do you know what they do with crazy people? They send them to college. During eight years of therapy with a psychologist, the state of Illinois helped me get a GED and sent me to college. Let me tell you, there is only one thing worse than an alcoholic. It's an educated alcoholic. I studied psychology with the idea of curing all you hopeless drunks and addicts. I remember thinking that one day, I would write a book exposing AA for what it really was: a bunch of weak people who can't make it on their own, supporting each other's self-pity, and using gallows humor to make light of what they've done. Boy, was I in for a big surprise when I had to come here." That tickles their funny bone. Since most of them know I write books about recovery based on the twelve steps, the irony doesn't escape them.

"I didn't drink for eight years, although I must admit that I did smoke some pot and took some pills. And I started therapy about the time a new psychological study was released saying that through psychotherapy, those with drinking problems could be taught new coping skills and learn to drink like normal human beings. Sounded good to me. So, throughout those years, I knew I would drink again."

I pause to think what number husband I'm on. "Right before I graduated, I got married again. Number four whisked me and my son off to Florida. It didn't last a month. My kid, his dog, myself, and two suitcases ended up in Sullivan, Illinois. I borrowed a truck, went back to Florida with a friend to get my stuff . . . such as it was. Sitting in a nice seafood restaurant, my friend said she might have a glass of wine. Why not, I thought, and that was the beginning of the end for me. Not the end of my marriages, not the end of my tragedies, but a fast road back to where I'd been when I hit bottom before."

Bracing myself, wishing I could stand behind the podium to have something to hold on to, I say, "Throughout my self-centered life, I dragged my poor son with me, in and out of drunken escapades, different men coming and going, moving here and there, always being on the run, with no affiliation to family or lasting friends. Even during those years of not drinking, I was so wrapped up in myself I couldn't see past my own nose to the fact that Jon was having problems. When it became so obvious that I had to recognize it, in my arrogance, I believed I could handle things. I was educated, you know. I made a real mess of things."

Focusing on a young, blond-headed boy sitting close to the front of the room, pushing past the pain welling up from deep inside, I continue. "He started asking about his father. I'd lied to him all his life, telling him his dad didn't want him. The real reason his dad wasn't in his life was because when I divorced him, I told him as long as he didn't bother me or Jon, I would never ask him for a penny. He agreed. It wasn't Jon he didn't want, it was me, and I used my son to punish him. I kept the lie going. But Jon, like most kids of a certain age, wanted to find him, to see him for himself. At age 15, already addicted to marijuana and booze, Jon stole a car. He was going to Arizona and search for his father. He got caught."

God, I hate talking about this part of my life, about what a miserable failure I was as a parent. "The next time I saw him was in a jail. Dressed in an orange jumpsuit, scared and desperate, he begged me to help him. I knew the sheriff and one of the local judges. After meeting with them and Jon's appointed attorney, a deal was made. If he'd agree to go to a treatment center approved by the judge, they would give him probation."

Assuring myself I can get through it this time without crying, I say, "He ran away from the treatment center less than two months after I took him there. He wouldn't have stayed that long, but he broke his leg. As soon as the cast was off, so was he. He hitched to Florida, where he had a friend, and then he called me. I did everything I could to talk him into returning to the treatment center, but he wasn't having it. He'd broken probation and would have to spend some time in jail. The plan, he said, was to hitch to Arizona. I begged him not to do it—told him to wait a few days until I could contact my brother in Phoenix and round up some cash for a bus ticket.

"I remember that phone call like it was yesterday. Jon told me he loved me, that he wasn't running away from me, but that he couldn't come back. My brother picked him up. He called, wanting me to join him in Arizona. I don't know how many times I've wondered what would have happened if I'd gone there to be with him—but I didn't. Instead, that day when I hung up the phone, I said a prayer. I hadn't prayed in years, since the kids and Mom died, and even then, I had no idea who or what I was praying to. But I looked into the air, and said, 'God, I can't take care of him anymore. Please look after him.'"

The tears come. I take a moment before I continue. "A few days later, there was a knock on the door. Jon was dead."

25

The Basement

YEARS HAVE PASSED, but still when I say those words out loud, I feel like I've been gut punched. For a moment, there's not enough air in the room. I catch my breath. "I heard a speaker say that if you are an alcoholic that has hit bottom, and you drink again, be assured you'll find the basement. I found the basement that day. There were no steps leading downward. The door opened, I fell in, and I landed on a concrete floor. I spent the next year lying in my own mess, drunk, filled with self-pity, believing I wanted to die."

I can barely recall that entire year. "The following summer, I met Cheryl. Actually, she followed me home from the liquor store, and I kept her." Good, they're laughing again. It brings me out of those dark thoughts. "What I mean is she helped me come back to life, such as it was. She became my best drinking buddy, and through her I met my next husband." I look at my watch and decide I can't afford to go into details about husband number five. "What a nice guy. He certainly deserved better than he got with me. By then, I had the drama queen martyr persona down to an art form. I'd played it so long, I believed in it myself. I truly felt that my life had been cursed, that none of it was my fault, and that someone should throw me a parade or give me an award for all I'd endured.

"My new husband didn't live up to my expectations. All I wanted him to do was put up with my bad habits, fill the loneliness that I'd lived with all my life, and help me get over Tom, the guy I'd been in love with for fifteen years. I don't know what his problem was. I drank every day and excused myself by blaming him. At times, I picked fights with him so I'd have a reason to go out, get blitzed, and do unthinkable things.

"After one of those nights, which ended in a blackout, I came to when I heard someone pounding on the door. It was Cheryl. She was upset. She started in on me as soon as I opened the door. Since I couldn't remember anything from the night before, I had no idea what she was yelling about. She said I had a drinking problem. I was stunned. I went into a rage, called her names, and threw her out. I thought she had a lot of nerve. After she left, I began to wonder. I couldn't get her words out of my mind. I tried drinking them away. By afternoon, I was sitting in the middle of my living room floor, rocking back and forth, knowing I was teetering on the edge of insanity.

"I used to say that I was more afraid of insanity than death, but that wasn't true. Thoughts of suicide had been with me since childhood. I fantasized about it. It had to be dramatic, creative, memorable—something people would talk about. My big problem was that there was no one left who would really give a damn, except for Tom, and maybe Cheryl. When Mom did it, people noticed, but they moved on with their lives pretty quickly, including me. And, as much as I tried to convince my-self that in death I'd be united with those I'd lost, it was too much of a crapshoot."

My eyes rest on a young woman near the front of the room whom I've worked with off and on over the past few years. We've recently had the "I wish I could just lay down and die" conversation—a few weeks ago. We laughed together when I told her we alcoholics were always looking for an easier, softer way. "I'd failed at everything I ever did. What if I screwed sui-cide up, too? I could end up paralyzed, or crippled, sucking my food through a straw in some state institution. No . . . too chancy."

I see her shoot me a knowing smile, and understand she's thinking about our last talk. A therapist once told me that the most profound thing I could say to someone who was suicidal was that I would miss them. I understood that. It's important to believe that if we fall off the face of the Earth, someone will care, someone will miss us. "Since apparently death wasn't an option—it was way too permanent—I chose what I considered to be just above death: jail and the nuthouse. I made the call.

"Jack answered it. He asked me if I could stay sober that day. There was a meeting that evening. No problem. I had a drink in my hand as soon as I hung up." I share the story of how I met Jack at the Amish catastrophe, then say, "Yes, I'd been speaking with a group of people about addiction and then going out and getting drunk. How crazy was that?" That story nearly brings the house down. I see people wiping at their eyes.

"I'll probably never forget my first encounter with the twelve steps. The word 'God' in some of the steps might as well have been written in florescent orange. That's all I could see. I didn't care if it was a God of your understanding, my understanding, or some church. I didn't want anything to do with it. If there was a God, he'd done nothing but crap on my life from the beginning. Except for a brief time in my life when my mother found out she had an incurable disease and decided to get religion (which consisted of going to church and switching to pills and vodka because someone told her no one could smell it), I'd pretty much been a heathen. No, this AA stuff wouldn't work for me. I don't think I'd ever needed a drink any worse than I did after that meeting. I got stinking drunk.

"There is nothing worse than a belly full of booze and a head full of AA. Those doubts, the ones that creep in under your denial radar, haunted me. By morning, facing the woman in the mirror, I knew I'd go to another meeting. I'm not sure why I made that choice. The one thing I remembered from the meeting was an old guy saying, 'You never have to be alone again.' Maybe that was enough. I'd never been alone in the sense that I had Jon, many husbands, live-ins, boyfriends, even Johns, to keep me from it, but I'd lived with an overwhelming feeling of loneliness all my life. Besides, I'd run out of anyplace else to go—at least anyplace I would be welcome. Even my best friend had abandoned me."

——

After all these years, that moment of truth lives in my mind like it was yesterday. "I grabbed a hold of that first step for dear life, and hung on by my fingernails. I left my husband, telling myself it was because I knew I couldn't live with him and stay sober, but the fact was that I'd been looking for an excuse to leave the marriage. I went to a meeting every night." I laugh out loud. "I asked one of the guys at the meeting how many meetings a week I should attend. He asked me how many days a week I drank. That settled that. It's funny, I didn't like the people, thought I was so much smarter than most of them, hated what they talked about in the meetings, resented the fact that so many meetings took place in churches, but I felt drawn to return night after night.

"I didn't understand the Higher Power business. The only Higher Power I'd ever known came in one bottle or another, or in a pair of tight blue jeans. Since I'd decided not to have a God of anyone's choosing, no matter what they called it, and was determined not to work any of the steps that mentioned God, I started out stuck on the first step. You can stay sober a long time on the first step. Sometimes I think I got the program through osmosis. As resistant as I was, I suited up and showed up, as they say, and apparently some of it seeped into my closed mind.

I had nothing. I always wondered why other people had so much and I had so little. They probably didn't live the way I did, moving fast and often, many times just ahead of the law and the landlord. I thought that if you couldn't get it in your car, you probably didn't need it. Not conducive to acquiring much. Anyway, I moved into a half-garage with my meager belongings and my son's dog, Angel. I didn't have a television, a radio, telephone, or an air conditioner. One good thing about that was that for the first time in my life, I had no distractions, and getting out of that place, even to attend meetings, was a treat."

It's funny, but when a girlfriend called recently to tell me they'd torn down the old garage, I felt sad. "Unlike many of you who have been given the opportunity to live in a treatment center . . . where they have drugs, I might add, I went through the DT's alone, except for those people in AA . . . you know, the ones I didn't like, who were kind enough to help me out. I shook. I suffered through the alcoholic itch, which was like having crabs all over my body. The AA people called me 'the pacer' because I couldn't sit down during the meetings. For over a year, I had insomnia, except when I was at work and I had trouble keeping my eyes open. It felt like I had the flu every day. My energy level was zip. I tried to substitute sugar for the loss of alcohol, but I think my body noticed.

In the mental hospital, where they didn't advocate a 12-step program, they gave me sugar, sugar, sugar. I developed such a sugar habit, I gained over thirty pounds. I was a sight: fat, my hair falling out, and what little I had left turning kind of orange-colored. Once, after my release, I ran into an old acquaintance from my drinking days. He didn't recognize me, and when he did he asked why my face was so swelled up. I would have dyed my hair brown, but I would have had to spray paint the bald spots. Although I couldn't do much about the hair except hope it would grow back in, I knew the solution to my weight. I smoked cigarettes one after the other, took diet pills, and ate one meal a day. That's how we alcoholics roll," I say, and can't keep from laughing along with the crowd.

"I always looked for the quick fix; the easier, softer way. It never worked for long, but I kept trying, moving from one disaster to the next, doing the same things and expecting different results. The question was: could I change that pattern? Was I willing to stop and make a real commitment?"

26

Limbo

"I BALANCED ON A TIGHTROPE between the sober world and the oblivion I craved through alcohol and drugs, knowing that at any moment I could fall. I brought my body to the meetings, but my mind continued to live in the bars. Hell, I didn't think they could run those places without me." I see some heads nodding in agreement.

"I'd been a con artist all my life, and that person still lived within. It remained in control of my brain, trying to fool me. I decided I was smart enough to figure out my way around this step stuff, you know, and just pretend to work the steps to keep up appearances. Like a zombie, I stared into the faces of those who were trying to help me, nodded, and thought, 'not me, baby. I don't have to actually work any of those steps—I just have to appear to do so.' Like all the other cons in my life, doing this made me feel smarter, more in control. But the only person duped in that particular con was me.

"When they say half measures avail you nothing, they aren't shitting you. I staged my apartment to fool those AA people who stopped by occasionally." In my mind, I picture the stupid things I did in an effort to make it look like I was working a program. "I taped three prayers to my bathroom mirror, made little signs that mimicked those sayings on the meeting room walls, and tacked them here and there. There was a partial list of people to whom I owed amends taped to the front of the refrigerator. When anyone mentioned God or a Higher Power, I told them I used the group as my Higher Power. I'd heard someone say that at a meeting. That worked for a while. What I didn't realize then was that was exactly what I had been doing."

Before I start the next part of my story, I'm on the verge of tears. I've never been able to talk about Helen without blubbering all over myself. Maybe this time I can do it. "My job as a day-care worker for Helen, who had Parkinson's, hadn't turned out quite like I figured. As much as I'd told myself I'd never allow myself to really care that much for another person again, I loved her dearly. She helped me as much as the people in the program. There she was, crippled up, in pain, confined to a bed, but she had faith in some God that I could not understand. And she knew peace. She was the beginning of my wondering."

A sad laugh escapes to cover the sobs I've experienced before. "Her family paid me to look after her, but I needed her more than she needed me. Because of her, I started actually reading those prayers on the bathroom mirror. Because of her, I started thinking about those hurtful things I'd done to others. And because of her, my perception of God, of what faith was, began to slowly change. But Helen was going to die. I told myself I could deal with it, but my mind worked furiously, telling me I knew how to smother the pain.

"A priest in recovery once told me that anything that causes you that much pain, that you hang on to that hard, you're getting something out of it. For me, my sadness over Helen's condition was an excuse to return to the bottle, to my self-destructive behavior, and justify it. As Helen deteriorated physically, I deteriorated emotionally. Although I'd begun playing with the steps, even making some half-assed efforts, I'd never stopped thinking about drinking as an option. Another great loss in my life would be the perfect excuse to start up again.

"For over two and a half years I'd lived in limbo—or so I thought. My life consisted of working, going to meetings, hanging out with AA people, fighting the urge to see Tom and the urge to drink and drug on a daily basis. When Helen ended up in the hospital, my world turned upside down. Forced to accept the reality of her inevitable demise, a plan formed in my mind. One morning, I got out of bed and knew that that was the day I would drink again. I went to work and took care of Helen, knowing all day that as soon as I got home and cleaned up, I'd go uptown and hit the bars.

"The plan worked pretty good until I stepped into the doorway on my way out of the garage. A voice came into my mind. Oh, it wasn't some big booming voice of God, but the words of a man—a man who I didn't like, because I felt he could see right through my bullshit. He'd looked straight into my face one day at a meeting and told me that the day would come when I would either get on my knees or get drunk. I had a two-word thought for him, I can tell you. But that day, I dropped to my knees. I begged for help. I didn't see a burning bush, or a white light, or even an angel, but such a feeling came over me—a feeling like nothing I'd ever known. It was as if someone wrapped me in a warm embrace and whispered in my ear, 'everything will be okay.'"

That familiar bubble of happiness fills me as it does every time I think of that day. "It was that one moment in time, that single action, that allowed me to enjoy the life I have today. I'd been told that if I do something today that works for me, it will work tomorrow. I know some of you won't believe this, but from that day to this, I still get on my knees each morning. That way, I get to have a spiritual awakening every day.

"I didn't know what God's will for me was, but I sure knew what it wasn't. Finally able to work the steps, I began the process of building the steps that led me out of the basement, one at a time. I discovered there is a reason the steps are numbered and set up the way they are. It's because each step prepares you for the next. This business of using the group as my Higher Power worked for me in the beginning, but what would I do when it was just me and the bottle, and there was no one else around? How would I have the courage to take responsibility for my past—and put it out there—without truly believing that there is a plan, and I'm part of it? For me, and I'm only speaking from my personal experience, there was no way to go forward without working steps 2 and 3, without a God of my understanding to lean upon when things got tough.

"My sponsor used to tell me that if I wanted it all, I needed to do it all. All my life, I protected myself by saying I didn't need anyone. The truth was that it wasn't that I didn't need them, but that I didn't think I could have them. I carried that person into the program, coming across like the typical macho broad, totally self-sufficient. But through my spiritual awakening, understanding I didn't have to walk through it alone, I became willing to do whatever it took for recovery."

I smile as one particular day comes to mind. It happened right around Easter. I watched *The Ten Commandments* at Helen's house. As I watched Moses wander through the desert and struggle toward total surrender, I thought, Jesus Christ, even Moses only had to wander for forty days and forty nights. I'd been wandering for over thirty-five years. I'm tempted to share the story, but it smacks of religion and I don't want to offend anyone. "The hardest part of total surrender is turning over control of the outcome. However, considering my best efforts had me sitting in meetings, angry, sick, and scared, maybe it was time to let someone else give it a shot.

"One problem with this total surrender business is that you don't get to do it once and you're good to go. Just as sobriety is one day at a time, so is spirituality. I've heard many people say they'd gotten a second chance at life. For me, I looked at this as my only chance. If I screwed this up, my life was over."

I've got a ways to go, and time is running out. I say, "I will try to wrap this up in the time allowed, but if I go over, and anyone needs to leave, feel free." No one gets up to go. "I went after those steps like a dog with a bone, but soon realized it had taken half my life to get to them, and they wouldn't be worked quickly. It was more important to do them thoroughly. It was agonizing, writing down all the stuff I'd done, people I'd hurt, saying out loud those shameful, disgusting secrets. The thought of forgiving and making amends to those who'd done some terrible things to me was overwhelming but necessary, according to my sponsor, if I was to ever know peace."

I remember having thoughts of giving it half measures. However, the big book says half measures will avail us nothing. It doesn't say we get a little peace. "I prayed for forgiveness from those who'd died, stood over graves talking to others, wrote letters and burned them, even tried writing messages, stuffing them into balloons, and releasing them to float into the heavens. As difficult as those things were, they were easier than looking a person in the eyes. I had a hell of a time making amends to Tom. Every time I saw him, I ended up getting angry and saying something else I'd have to make amends for. After speaking with a woman from the meetings about it, I knew what I'd have to do—not only admit to what I'd done, but to how I'd felt about him all those years.

"I did it. For the first time since I met him, I felt resolved, like I could put my feelings to rest, accept that I loved him but that we couldn't be together. I'd chosen a sober life, and he continued his drinking lifestyle. At home that night, I gave him to my Higher Power. He stopped calling me, so I figured I'd gotten my answer. Months passed as I pursued my steps with honesty and vigor. My situation hadn't changed, but I'd changed. I knew happiness, peace of mind, had attained a feeling of self-respect, and no longer had to fight the urge to drink or drug.

"I lived in a state of gratitude for every little thing in my life.

"As this God of mine had a way of doing, he threw me a curveball now and again just to shake things up. Tom called. He'd been sober for months, and wanted to know if I'd have a cup of coffee with him. Unsure what to do, I prayed about it, asking my Higher Power to let me know what direction to take. At the coffee shop, Tom pulled out his billfold to pay. It was the one Jon made for him when he was in Cub Scouts. At that moment, I knew Tom truly loved me. We were married a few months later, after Helen passed away, and have been happily married for over twenty years now. Talk about a miracle."

Like always, the great love I feel for Tom swells my heart until it's nearly bursting. I raise my arm. "It was like my life had been waiting for me all along, just out of reach, until I became willing to surrender. I know there are people in the meetings who think I'm so happy because of the life I share with Tom, the things I've accomplished over the years, but that's not true.

I found peace and happiness while living hand to mouth in that garage. I don't believe I could have ever been happy with another human being until I found it within myself first.

"Don't kid yourself that it will all be peaches and cream because you're sober. Life keeps happening. There will always be illness, death, financial problems, problems with family members, and God only knows what else. The difference is that with a program and a Higher Power, there will be solutions, if you are willing to use the tools. I have faltered many times, in particular when I went through a life-threatening illness. I wallowed in my self-pity for a short while, fell back into anger and resentment, but thank God and this program, I didn't drink, and found the willingness to get into action.

In sobriety, I had the opportunity to become a professional costumer. I opened my own rental shop, which thrived, and I was living the dream. My illness took all of that away. I was pissed. However, through that experience, I discovered the writer in me. Sometimes the gifts we receive come wrapped in strange packages. Tom and I moved to our small mountain community in Arizona as a place for me to heal and write. And, I might add, I finally got the opportunity to write that exposé about Alcoholics Anonymous, exposing it for what it really is." Laughter explodes through the room.

"To sum it up, I joined a program I thought was the height of stupidity, found a Higher Power I didn't think existed, worked steps I saw as ridiculous and impossible, ended up in the last place on earth I thought I would ever go again, married the one man I thought was out of my reach, and have lived long enough, stayed sober long enough, to see all the promises come true in my life—which still blows my mind. You just can't get here from where I started—without divine intervention. There was the life I thought I would live and the one my Higher Power had planned for me when I was ready to accept it. I like His better.

"I stand in awe of my life on a daily basis. Years ago, my sponsor told me that one day I would get to be the voice of joy. Well, here I am. I know joy, and I know if it is possible for someone like me, it can happen for you. So, when you wonder if it's worth the effort, I hope you'll think of me, and others like me, who worked those steps that allowed us to emerge from that dark place to a life beyond our wildest drunken dreams. Thank you for being here for me because without you, and others who have passed through my life, this program, and my Higher Power, I would not be the person I am. All that I am, all that I've accomplished, is a direct result of AA, the people in the program, and a God of my understanding. I will be forever grateful."

27

Full Circle

THE QUIET IS ASTOUNDING. Eyes closed, I listen to the whoosh of a raven's wings as he flies overhead and the water falling over the boulder behind the house as it rushes down the creek at the bottom of the hill. I feel the cool breeze ruffling my hair. I am taken back to another place, another time.

My therapist had hypnotized me. He asked me to return to the last time in my life that I felt safe. Images of myself down on the river with Grampa the summer before school started began to take shape. I loved being there with him. Others may have seen him as just another old man, but not me. He was my hero. He knew things, special things, like how to glean leaves, bark, and berries from the woods to use them for healing. He had the gift of removing warts through his touch. People used to come from all over to have their warts removed. He didn't say much, but somehow I always knew he would protect me no matter what.

Grampa tied a rope around my waist and threw me in the river to teach me to swim. He was of a mind that like in animals, swimming would be a natural instinct for me. I can't remember ever not knowing how to swim. When he made his secret fish bait, he allowed Bill and me to roll it into balls to be put on the trout lines. At dusk, in a rowboat, he'd glide through the muddy Kaskaskia River, sticking the smelly bait on each hook. As hard as it was to drag myself out from under the patchwork quilt on the feather bed Bill and I shared with Grampa and Alma before sunrise, I couldn't wait to see what we'd caught. Sometimes there would be a turtle or a big old salamander, instead of the typical catfish, carp, or buffalo fish dangling on the line.

Grampa's gentleness, his ability to tame a wild animal like our pet raccoon, Susie, or the squirrel who would eat out of his hand, amazed me. He would go off hunting sometimes, but never killed anything we weren't going to eat. I suppose we were poor, if you counted money, but I didn't know it until we lived in town, I started school, and other kids made fun of me. We always had plenty to eat, a warm place to sleep, a world of interesting things to do, and the Thompson Mill covered bridge that stretched across the river and gave rise to many of my childhood fantasies.

My favorite spot was a creaky old porch swing tied between two trees with ropes. It was heaven to lie in the shade, look at the bridge, hear the soft ripple of the river flowing over the rock dam that Grampa, my dad, and his brothers built, and daydream. At times, between the movement of the swing to and fro and the squeak of the ropes, I'd drift off into wonderful, fanciful dreams.

Often, after I got older and life bore down on me, I'd imagine returning to the river, where I would build a cabin and find the peace I'd long ago lost. I traveled there from time to time. It was never the same. The cabin and outhouse had been torn down, the swing was gone, the cornfields that had been my perfect hiding place from Grandma Alma, who'd never liked me much, barren and sad. Besides, the property was bought by my dad's brother, the stepfather who disliked me intensely. He'd remarried after Mom died, and finally had the family he wanted—not a couple of worthless brats like my brother and me.

The last time I traveled to the river, the State of Illinois had constructed a concrete bridge parallel to the covered bridge, which was being conserved for its historical value. I stood at the foot of the new bridge, right where our cabin used to sit, watched the cars zip across the arched concrete monstrosity, and knew I'd never go back again.

Today, sitting here on the front deck of our oddly shaped house that wanders up the side of the mountain amongst the boulders and scrub oaks, I understand it's not the river I missed, but how I felt there that I'd been trying to recapture all my life: the quiet; my childhood innocence; freedom; no worry about how others saw me, what they thought of me; but most of all, the simple life.

Now, I have it. Like Dorothy in *The Wizard of Oz,* one of my all-time favorite movies, the solution had been with me all along. But like Dorothy, I had to overcome a lot of obstacles to find my way home. My personal yellow brick road began the day I walked into my first 12-step meeting.

In early sobriety I lived in forced simplicity. There were homeless people, people who lived in cars, that had more possessions than I did. And they probably had friends. Through my addictions and behavior, I'd lost everything, and everyone. At age 35, alone and sick in more ways than one, I resented having to start over yet again with no buffer between me and a cruel world. Today, I know it was an essential part of my journey.

Last night at the meeting in Congress, a small town at the foot of the mountains, I picked up my 26-year sobriety chip, blew out the candles on the cake, and shared part of my story. I laughed when I said, "I think God looked at me, shook his head, and thought there was nothing left to do but take me down to nothing and start over," but somewhere deep inside, I believed it. It wasn't until I discovered how little I knew that I could open myself to the possibilities of my life.

By the time Tom and I married twenty-three years ago, I'd learned what it meant to carry the river in my heart wherever I went, through whatever I was doing, with whomever was with me. Since then, I've become that little girl again: the one who loves completely, knows trust, awakens each morning ready to explore a new and exciting day, and finds joy in the smallest things. She'd been struggling to get out all my life, and the twelve steps gave me the tools needed to mend my ravaged mind and heart. My body didn't fare quite so well, but I'm impressed that it's still up and walking around, considering what I've put in it and done to it. I'm officially twice as old as I, or anyone who knew me back then, ever thought I'd be.

———

Tom is coming up the road, our two new dogs on long leashes, darting here and there. My heart beats a little faster, swells with a warm, comfortable love that reminds me of the day I first fell into the embrace of a God of my understanding. I always get maudlin this time of year as I reflect on my life. Sometimes, I feel like great streams of light rainbows and bubbles will burst forth from my body because I can no longer contain my joy.

Kahlil Gibran said, "The deeper sorrow carves into your soul, the more joy you can contain." His words flash through my mind as Tom joins me on the deck, hands me a cup of coffee, and leans against the railing to gaze out at the landscape. He says, "How in the world did we ever end up here?"

"Maybe it was a God thing," I respond.

"You think?" he says, and laughs. "I know it wasn't my idea." He'd always said that when he retired, we'd move to the country outside his hometown in St. Elmo, Illinois, build a cabin, raise hounds, and do some quail hunting. That was the plan.

I, on the other hand, never figured I'd live long enough to retire—and on the off chance that I did, I imagined myself working until I dropped dead. I certainly wasn't planning on doing that in Arizona, where so many bad things happened in my life. There was a better chance that I'd see my picture on a post office bulletin board than that I'd end up here, writing books on recovery, happy and reasonably healthy, having a real life. God must have had a big belly laugh while we were making plans.

When Tom goes into the house to get a piece of cake I brought home from last night's meeting, I can hold back no longer. Overwhelmed with gratitude, silent tears roll down my cheeks. Raising my face to the cloudless turquoise sky, I whisper, "Thank you for everything." And I mean everything. I know it has taken every moment, all my experiences, good and seemingly bad, and every individual who passed through my life to bring me to this moment in time, to the person I am today. I've come full circle, back to the little girl on the porch swing full of hopes and dreams, who at the end of the day knelt by her bed, hands pressed together, whispering, "Now I lay me down to sleep, I pray the Lord my soul to keep. If I die before I wake, I pray the Lord my soul to take."

About the Author

Barb Rogers learned most of her life lessons through great pain and tragedy. After surviving abuse, the death of her children, addiction, and life-threatening illness, she succeeded in finding a new way of life. She became a professional costume designer and founded Broadway Bazaar Costumes. When an illness forced her to give up costume designing, Barb turned to writing. She is the author of three costuming books and several titles on recovery, alcoholism and addiction, and well-being, including: *Twenty-Five Words, Keep It Simple and Sane,* and *Clutter-Junkie No More.* Barb lives in Arizona with her husband and their two dogs.

To Our Readers

Conari Press, an imprint of Red Wheel/Weiser, publishes books on topics ranging from spirituality, personal growth, and relationships to women's issues, parenting, and social issues. Our mission is to publish quality books that will make a difference in people's lives—how we feel about ourselves and how we relate to one another. We value integrity, compassion, and receptivity, both in the books we publish and in the way we do business.

Our readers are our most important resources, and we value your input, suggestions, and ideas about what you would like to see published. Please feel free to contact us, to request our latest book catalog, or to be added to our mailing list.

Conari Press
An imprint of Red Wheel/Weiser, LLC
500 Third Street, Suite 230
San Francisco, CA 94107
www.redwheelweiser.com